contents

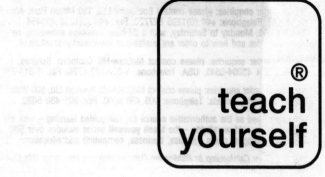

iPods and iTunes

peter cope

for over 60 years, more than 50 million people have learnt over 750 subjects the **teach yourself** way, with impressive results.

be where you want to be with **teach yourself**

For UK orde enquiries, please contact Bookpoint Ltd, Milton Park, ingdon, Oxon OX14 4SB. Telephone: +44 (0)1235 827720. Fax: +44 (0)1235 400454. nes are open 09.00–17.00 Monday to Saturday, with a 24-hour message answering rvice. Details about our tit s and how to order are available at www.teachyourself.co.uk

For USA ord enquiries: please contact McGraw-Hill Customer Services PO Box 545, Blacklick, OH 43004-0545, USA. Telephone: 1-800-722-4726. Fax: 1-614 755-5645.

For Canada o der enquiries: please contact McGraw-Hill Ryerson Ltd, 300 Water St, Whitby, Ontario L1N 9B6, Canada. Telephone: 905 430 5000. Fax: 905 430 5020.

Long renown d as the authoritative source for self-guided learning – with more than 50 million copie sold worldwide – the teach yourself series includes over 500 titles in the fields of lang ages, crafts, hobbies, business, computing and education.

British Library Cataloguing in Publication Data: a catalogue record for this title is available from The British Library.

Library of Congress Catalog Card Number: on file.

First published in UK 2007 by Hodder Education, 338 Euston Road, London NW1 3BH.

First published in US 2007 by The McGraw-Hill Companies, Inc.

The **teach yourself** name is a registered trademark of Hodder Headline.

Computer hardware and software brand names mentioned in this book are protected by their respective trademarks and are acknowledged.

Typeset by MacDesign, Southampton

Printed in Great Britain for Hodder Education, a division of Hodder Headline, an Hachette Livre UK Company, 338 Euston Road, London NW1 3BH, by Cox & Wyman Ltd, Reading, Berkshire.

The publisher has used its best endeavours to ensure that the URLs for external websites referred to in this book are correct and active at the time of going to press. However, the publisher and the author have no responsibility for the websites and can make no guarantee that a site will remain live or that the content will remain relevant, decent or appropriate.

Hodder Headline's policy is to use papers that are natural, renewable and recyclable products and made from wood grown in sustainable forests. The logging and manufacturing processes are expected to conform to the environmental regulations of the country of origin.

Impression number	10 9 8 7 6 5 4 3 2 1
Year	2011 2010 2009 2008 2007

'Mr Watson, come here! I need you!' When those seminal words, that comprised the very first phone call, were spoken by Alexander Graham Bell to his assistant Thomas Watson, Watson could hardly have appreciated the profound effect of the communications tool used to summon him would have upon the whole world. Even Mr Bell would, we think, have been surprised.

There must have been something of a sense of déjà vu when, in October 2001, Steve Jobs of Apple Computers first demonstrated the iPod to a select audience. For Steve and his colleagues the importance of the diminutive device they were about to launch was clear; to the audience perhaps less so. After all, Bell's first practical application of the telephone quickly launched an unambiguous revolution in communications. The iPod was just a digital music player of which (even in these early days of digital music) there were many other examples.

What was it that made the iPod and its companion digital music library software application iTunes into a true global phenomenon? The original reception was lukewarm: industry pundits were expecting something more glamorous from the company that had given the world the Macintosh (and, controversially inspired the interfaces used by almost all computers) than a mere pocket jukebox. Even those that might have seen some of the potential would have been disheartened to discover that the original offering (and that offered for sale for some time thereafter) would only be made available to the comparatively small pool of Macintosh users.

Confounding the pundits, this unique combination of a player and software so perfectly matched was clearly a system whose time had come. Marrying a convenient, simple-to-use player with software that was equally simple to use gave mass-market appeal. Bring on the Windows version and success was assured. Sales and the popularity of the iPod have been such that even the name has become synonymous with digital music players. Along with similar devices from other manufacturers it took its place in a vibrant market, becoming the premier must-have gadget for many years running.

Not one to rest on the deserved laurels however, Apple went on to consolidate its position by a process of continual product development. The original iPod grew both in capacity and scope. Though maintaining the spiritual music basis, iPods began to act as repositories for digital photos and video too. The increasingly incongruously named iTunes added a store through which you could purchase not only music tracks but also music videos and then full-length movies.

Commuters were no longer limited to listening to their music collections but could catch up on their favourite episodes of TV dramas or even news bulletins in the form of podcasts. Pundits who argued that the diminutive screen of the iPod was too small for watching video have been confounded as TV drama and even feature-length movies are now likely to share space with music on a typical iPod and be enjoyed on the move.

Apart from raw sales (which are themselves impressive and continue to grow beyond the 100 million sold in the first five years) the iPod has had another effect on our world. Once it was a measure of our wealth (musical or financial) to give prominence to a collection of CDs in our homes. Visitors could browse the collection and be given pointers to the hosts' musical tastes. Heavy rock or eclectic? Jazz or classical?

Now that hundreds – perhaps thousands – of CDs can be stored on our computer and an iPod, those prized original CDs – like tape cassettes and vinyl albums before them – have been consigned to garages and attics. Now it is the technology, rather than the music, that takes pride of place.

So your iPod is now a photo album... video player... and more. The onward march continues: the iPhone. An iPod with mobile phone capabilities? Or a phone with music replay facilities? Or something new altogether? Whatever the answer, in the world of digital music – or perhaps we should say digital media – nothing stands still for long.

Conventions and descriptions

Despite the iPod and iTunes being a product of Apple Inc., creator of the Macintosh computer system, there are actually far more iPods in the hands of Windows users than Mac users. So throughout this book we tend not to discriminate against one in favour of the other. We use both Windows computers and Macintoshes when we describe features. Often the software is identical and where there are distinct differences we'll clearly say so.

Also the instructions and advice given in this book may sometimes vary slightly from that which applies to your iPod. This is especially true if you use earlier software versions. In these cases, please use the advice given here as guidance only and refer to the specific instructions that relate to your model or version.

The best thing about digital music is the freedom it affords. Music collections that were once confined, by virtue of their weight and size, to our homes can now travel with us anywhere. Add in your photo and video library too and your whole world can travel with you. Let's learn how to make the best of it.

In this book we tend to use the term 'iPod' generically but also specifically to describe the original iPod and its descendants, all the way down to today's iPod classic.

01 choosing your iPod

In this chapter you will learn:

- about the range of iPod models
- about the history of iTunes
- about the capabilities of different models
- which iPod model is best for you

If you've chosen to read this book you'll be falling into one of two camps. In one will be those of you who have an iPod and want to get more from it. You'll probably have been using it to listen to music but probably have done little else. In the other camp will be those who have decided the time has come to get your first iPod. You may have some form of digital music player already, or you may be graduating from an old CD Walkman, tape player or even, nothing at all.

In this chapter we will take a look at the iPod family, including taking a brief look at some of the range's ancestors. For those aiming to buy their first iPod, it will help you choose which model is best for you; if you are already enjoying the benefits then you'll hopefully find out more about what your particular model can do. We'll take a look too at the parallel evolution of the iPod's companion software, iTunes.

First let's go back to basics. What is a digital music player? For our purposes here, that's the iPod. It's a device that can store, organize and play digital music files. It's sometimes also called an MP3 player, though, as we'll shortly see, this is (certainly in the case of an iPod) incorrect. Digital music players store music (and any audio) in digital form using special techniques to compress more music on to the player than we could achieve if we were using the original files from a CD, or recordings made from tape or disc.

Your iPod will be one of two types:

A flash-based player: these have no moving parts (except, if you are being particularly pedantic, any user-operated switches) with the music stored on flash-based memory chips, in much the same way that files can be saved on a USB keydrive. These chips retain anything written on them even when switched off and even if any power connection is removed. The smaller iPods, the mini, shuffle and nano are traditionally of this type,

A hard disc player: for higher capacities, flash-based memory tends to get expensive and so it's often more effective to use a small hard drive, of the type you might find in a laptop computer. Though they lead to larger devices, they do have much larger capacities. The original iPod and its successors are of this type.

Evolution of the species

The iPod first saw the light of day, in 2001. Few, except perhaps those in the inner circle at Apple, appreciated what the future would be like. Since then the iPod has evolved through several generations and, with each, gained new features and functionality. Remarkably, and as a testament to the purity of the original design, most of the changes over the years have been evolutionary rather than revolutionary: only in the details can you spot the differences. Here's the iPod spotter's guide:

First generation

The scroll wheel model and the original. Launched in October 2001, it comprised a white-only model with a hard disc drive of 5 or 10GB capacity. Below the monochrome screen was the signature wheel that, unlike successive models, actually rotated for accessing menu items. An additional ring of buttons were used to access the secondary controls. Connection, for charging and downloading music, was via a FireWire cable and a FireWire socket on the iPod.

Second generation

Launched in July 2002, the similar-sized model sported a 10 or 20GB hard disc. The monochrome screen remained the same but the scroll wheel was replaced with a new touch-sensitive design. The control buttons were moved from around the wheel to just below the screen. Again, connectivity was provided by FireWire. This time there was a Windows version (it had been Macintosh only to this point) although it did not ship with the companion iTunes music library/management system but with Yahoo MusicMatch. Ads in the trade press suggested a Windows version of

Second generation iPod: the most visibly different of iPods, because of the row of four buttons below the screen.

iTunes was coming: Apple was advertising for programmers with Windows expertise. iTunes for Windows finally surfaced in October 2003.

Third generation

The most significant change to this model, released in April 2003, was the change from a FireWire socket to the now standard dock connector. This still used FireWire for connection to the computer. At the same time the opportunity was taken to introduce a new, larger capacity 30GB model.

iPod mini: the first generation

Not a replacement, but a junior sibling. With a compact design, and an anodized aluminium body the iPod mini was offered in different colours: silver, gold, pink, blue and green. This diminutive body contained a small 4GB microdrive. This was a mini hard disc that was designed for use, originally, in devices such as digital cameras, where the hard drive was a cheaper alternative to the CompactFlash memory card. Like its second-generation successor, it sported a dock connector.

The iPod mini introduced the click wheel with the function buttons included on the wheel itself. Grey lettering on the click wheel characterized first-generation iPod minis which made its debut in January 2004.

Fourth generation

The iPod mini's older brother got a makeover in July 2004 and adopted the same click wheel with buttons design from the mini. Unlike the mini, the body remained white with a monochrome display. Hard disc sizes increased to 20 or 40GB.

iPod Photo: a minor tweak to the fourth-generation iPod brought a colour screen and the ability to store and display images.

A black version with red click wheel was released at around the same time, called the U2 Special Edition. As the name suggests, it was the result of a tie-up with the band U2. Apart from the unique colour scheme, the Special Edition sported the signatures of the band members engraved on the back. It came with a voucher to enable the downloading of the band's music collection from the iTunes Music Store. This version was updated, with a colour display in June 2005.

In October 2004, an intermediate upgrade added a colour display and an increase in capacity to either 40 or 60GB. The iPod could now also store photos. A 30GB model was added in February 2005 and 20 and 60GB black models in the following July.

iPod mini: second generation

February 2005: a modest upgrade saw the capacity increase by 50% to 6GB. The keen-eyed iPod spotter will also point out that the button icons on the click wheel have now been changed to the same colour as the body.

iPod shuffle: first generation

The long-rumoured basic iPod surfaced at the start of 2005, dubbed the iPod shuffle. Why? With no display to help navigate the onboard music library the suggestion was that you'd play a random selection of your favourite tracks. With modest capacities of 512MB and 1GB it was not designed for storing your entire music collection (as the full size models were) and was promoted (with accessories such as an action case) for people to use at the gym and out jogging. There was no dock connector – instead, a USB plug concealed under an end cap could be used to connect directly to a computer's USB socket.

iPod nano: first generation

September 2005 saw the appearance of the third-generation iPod mini. Or rather, it didn't. Though the iPod mini was a runaway success it was replaced with the even more compact iPod nano, complete with colour screen and click wheel. Distinguishing it from the mini, the nano featured flash memory (that is, solid state memory card, as you might find in a phone or camera) in capacities of 2 and 4GB. A 1GB model was released in the following February. Now the connectivity (via the dock) was USB only. FireWire connections were on the way out. Colours? No, just black or white, high gloss finish.

Fifth generation

Away from the action with the nano and shuffle, the iPod itself became the iPod Video in October 2005. With a choice of black or white body, larger colour screen (within a similar sized body to previous generations) the iPod Video had 30 or 60GB hard discs and the dock connection via USB only, as with the nano.

September 2006: this model was essentially about making a good thing better. The high resolution colour display was improved (in particular offering better brightness), it became thinner, had a longer battery life and added a music search function. Capacities were now 30, 60 or 80GB.

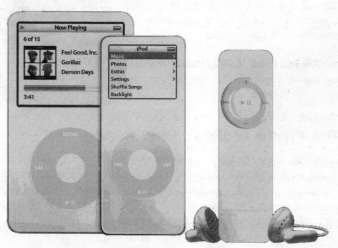

The iPod Family Portrait, 2005: featuring the fifth-generation iPod, iPod nano and iPod shuffle (both in first-generation guise).

iPod nano: second edition

With the sixth generation iPod came the second generation of the iPod nano. In the same form and size as the original, the new models featured a similar anodized aluminium body to the iPod mini. Capacities were enhanced (2, 4 and 8GB) as was battery life and the body was offered in black, silver, pink, green or blue (though not all capacities were available in all colours).

iPod nano: a plastic fascia gives way to more durable aluminium.

iPod shuffle: second generation

Following on closely in October 2006 came the second generation of the iPod shuffle. Smaller still (considerably so) it offered 1GB of memory, similar controls (with no display) and an integral belt/shirt clip. Coloured versions were also offered including a limited edition PRODUCT (RED)™ version to continue the U2 connection.

Shrinking Shuffle: the second-generation iPod shuffle was tiny but offered a similar audio performance to more senior members of the family.

The iPhone: an iPod ... and some

Rumours were rife for some years that Apple would get involved in the mobile phone business. Those rumours talked vaguely of something dubbed – in the popular press rather than from Apple itself – of an 'iPhone', a mobile phone that would boast Apple's unique take on simple operation and perhaps, just perhaps, offer some of the functionality of an iPod.

This idle chat was answered when, in 2005, Apple and mobile phone giant Motorola jointly announced the ROKR E1 mobile phone. The E1 was, for Apple, a fairly conventional mobile phone that had additional connectivity allowing a link to iTunes. So, as well as performing as a fully specified mobile phone it could be used to download a (limited) amount of music from your library. It's fair to say the E1 device had a lukewarm reception and lacked the euphoric accolades normally heaped on a new Apple product announcement. In fact, so muted was the response that many people began to speculate that this was very much an interim solution and that the fabled iPhone was yet to debut.

Rumours continued to grow but were rather eclipsed by tales of another must-have device, an iPod with a widescreen display. Speculators argued that given iTunes was now serving up high quality widescreen content, there must surely be a player on the horizon that could display it in its full glory.

Rumours reached fever pitch prior to the annual Macworld show in January 2007. In fact, things heated up to the point that there were expectations that possibly both a widescreen iPod and the iPhone would turn in an appearance. The rumours proved correct: both appeared, and in the same package. Announced as the iPhone (and causing a little anxiety because another company, Cisco had rights to the name), the new device was not only a new form of mobile phone but also the widescreen iPod. For good measure, it had a third string to its bow: it was an Internet communications device too.

As an iPod, the iPhone delivers all the functionality we had come to expect from the conventional designs but with a widescreen display that almost filled the face of the device, leaving no room for any controls. Pundits had argued that to combine the simple

The iPhone: after the false dawn of the ROKR E1 the iPhone proved a true and worthy member of the family.

effective control of an iPod with a wide screen could result in a device that was unwieldy. Apple avoided this by incorporating the controls (which are as simple as ever, if a bit more comprehensive) as elements on the touch sensitive screen. With a few flicks of the finger you can navigate your music library and see the music you've selected as album artwork on the display.

Better still, the display can also be configured to use CoverFlow. CoverFlow first appeared in version 7 of iTunes and allowed users to navigate their music collection by flicking though thumbnails of the album covers. The same technology is also used now in the Mac operating system OS X for scanning through files and documents. In the iPhone, under fingertip control, it allows quick access to selected music tracks.

The range refreshed

In September 2007, Apple introduced a refreshed range of iPods. The iPod shuffle saw the most modest of changes – a new range of colours. The iPod nano saw the most significant changes: a new shorter and wider format allowed the use of a larger screen. With this came the ability to play video, like its larger sibling (now dubbed the iPod Classic). It also came in the same colour range as the shuffle and in two capacities – 4GB and 8GB.

The iPod Classic retained the black-or-white finishes but gained larger hard discs: 80GB or 160GB. A modest change to the menu system (shared with the iPod nano) uses a split screen, displaying the menu to the left and graphics to the right.

Headlining the new range was the iPod Touch. Essentially an iPhone without the phone, the Touch has the same widescreen display, touch display and navigation system. Though it doesn't have phone facilities it does feature Wi-Fi web browsing (just like a wireless laptop) allowing access to a special version of the iTunes store for downloads and access to You Tube. It was launched with capacities of 8GB and 16GB.

iPod and iTunes – a dream team

From the outset, the iPod was never meant to be a stand-alone digital music player, it was to be the partner of a music software application to which it would be closely bound and with which

The iPod family: 2007 saw the first appearance of the iPod touch and the evolution of the iPod nano into a video model.

it would work in concert. That application, as you probably know, is called iTunes. But did you know that iTunes arrived some time ahead of the iPod? iTunes comprised one element of the iLife suite of programs supplied with all new Macintosh computers, along with iPhoto – a photo library and editing application and iMovie, arguably the easiest movie editing software ever devised (subsequently iDVD, a DVD authoring application, and iWeb, a simple web page creator, have been added). As well as being part of iLife, iTunes was also available (as it has been subsequently) as a free download from the Apple website.

Where's the iPod?

The original iTunes, which appeared in January 2001, had much of the look of the iTunes we know today but experienced iTunes users would notice quite a few differences. First of all, it was Mac only; there was no Windows version. Second, features such as the music store – which allow you to buy music, movies and video – were missing. In fact this was a simple application that let users rip their CDs (that is, import the music from a CD in a special, compact form) and store them in a library on the computer's hard disc. From there you could create playlists (sequences of tracks) and replay them through the computer. And that was about it.

An upgrade to iTunes in October 2001 added in the ability to synchronize with an iPod, although it was fair to say that at that time most people were more concerned with modest improvements to its functionality as a computer-based music player.

By the time version 3 appeared in 2002, it was clear that the iPod was not a passing fad; sales were beginning to pick up momentum and the sound of the sales was only drowned out by the demands from users of Windows computers to get a bit of the action. Not that they had not tried to circumvent the Mac-only lockout. Various software applications had tried to fool iPods and computers into working but the situation was only partially remedied with the release of the iTunes-less version of the iPod.

The legend grows

The writing was on the wall, or at least in the situations vacant columns, as Apple set about engineering a Windows version of iTunes. This was expected with version 4.0 of iTunes, released in October 2003. Instead, this offered some new and significant changes that were, for the moment, reserved for Mac users. The first was the introduction of the Apple Advanced Codec. This was a new way of storing digital music files that allowed very high quality reproduction but with compact file sizes.

MP3 and iPod

It's important to clear up a major misconception about digital music. We tend to call the digital version 'MP3' but the MP3 format is just one of many digital music formats and, arguably, not one of the best. It's been superseded by others, including AAC, that offer much better results.

The music store appears...

The other major advance in version 4 was the iTunes Music Store. This was a major step forward and a major coup for Apple. Until this time most of the digital music tracks passed around on the Internet were illegal copies. Apple, with iTunes and the iPod saw the opportunity of a legitimate music store where music would be favourably priced, making it affordable and a good alternative to the pirate and illegal sites. The iTunes Music Store was the fruit of those long labours.

... and so does Windows compatibility

The appearance of the store (albeit only for the US market at first) turned the desire for a Windows version into a clamour. So, with every ounce of publicity extracted from the store launch, Apple announced iTunes 4.1: for Mac and Windows.

iTunes Store: since its inception the iTunes Store has continued to flourish.

iTunes interface: version 7 of iTunes introduced CoverFlow, a flip-though way of viewing album covers and a format it shares with the original iPhone.

Subsequent releases of iTunes have added new functionality, some related with content (e.g. the ability to download videos, podcasts – subscription-based news and narratives – movies and TV programming) and others related to modifications and enhancements to the iPod. A summary of the principal changes, modifications and enhancements to iTunes is shown in Table 1.

Table 1 Changes, modifications and enhancements to iTunes

Version	Release date	Key changes/upgrades
Mac OS 9		
1.0	Jan 2001	Digital music player that predates the iPod
2.0	Oct 2001	Added features and compatibility with iPods
Mac OS 9 & X		
3.0	July 2002	Play counter and ratings added, along with OS X compatibility
4.0	April 2003	AAC format and Music Store added*
Mac OS 9 & X Windows		
4.1	Oct 2003	Windows compatibility added
4.7	Oct 2004	Support for iPod Photo added
4.8	May 2005	Support for video added
4.9	June 2005	Support for podcasting added
5.0	Sept 2005	New coding with new interface design
6.0	Oct 2005	Support for iPod video added
7.0	Sept 2006	Added games, album artwork and movie downloads
7.2	May 2007	DRM free music downloads (iTunes Plus) and iTunes U
7.4	Sept 2007	Compatibility with new iPods (inc. Touch), WiFi Store appears

Going for quality

In May 2007 the version 7.2 upgrade brought two more significant updates. iTunes U launched a new channel in iTunes dedicated to learning resources. Lessons and course material from some of the most renowned learning centres and universities were made available for the first time. More significantly for the general market, iTunes Plus launched. This provided even higher quality downloads, free of digital rights management software, but for a premium price.

What DRM is all about

Digital Rights Management (DRM) software is encoding within media tracks (music and video) that restricts the copying and distribution. This was regarded as essential for the big music labels to distribute music via iTunes and other stores to counter piracy. However it also limits what legitimate purchasers can do with their purchases. Apple's CEO and visionary Steve Jobs fought hard for the exclusion of DRM and the compromise was the sale of DRM-free tracks at a higher price. In exchange for that premium, downloaders could enjoy a higher quality track.

Do you need an iPod to get the most from iTunes? To enjoy your music collection plus music or media you've downloaded from the Music Store, yes, but you can still enjoy all the same on your computer.

Choosing an iPod

With so many models, and with clearly more to come, which will be best for you? See if you can recognize yourself from amongst the following categories and then find your perfect digital music companion.

I want to carry my large music collection with me everywhere – and some photos and movies too.

The largest capacity iPod: 80GB or more should be sufficient but larger capacities will ensure that you've enough space to accommodate any growth in your collection. As a very rough rule of thumb, 80GB will allow you to store 1500 hours of music (though any movie footage you carry will reduce that).

I've an average music collection and I want to carry it everywhere with me.

A standard iPod should be sufficient for your needs. 80GB will provide around 500 hours of storage – that's 1200 to 1500 standard albums.

I want something to let me enjoy music when commuting or travelling.

If you don't want to carry everything with you all the time you don't need a full-sized iPod. An iPod nano should be sufficient for all your needs. This will give you the capacity for several thousand songs but in a package that can easily be slipped in a pocket or handbag.

I need a player to take with me running and to the gym.

The iPod shuffle is lightweight and easily clipped to a gym belt, pocket or lapel. The capacity will be more than enough for a good few gym sessions.

I want to watch movies on the move.

Screen size comes to the fore: the latest standard iPods allow reasonable viewing size though the award for the largest screen goes to the iPod Touch and the iPhone.

I would like to carry my photo album with me everywhere.

An iPod will let you carry a large collection of photos with you – and provide a backup of your photo library too. An iPod nano will store thumbnails of your image collection if you aren't worried about having large-sized images with you all the time.

I need to be careful about how much I spend.

The shuffle is modestly priced but lacks a screen or large capacity. Spend around double that and you can get a nano. That's the perfect price/features compromise. Spend double that again and you'll be getting into the territory of the standard iPod.

I want to carry my music collection but need to keep in touch.

An iPhone, avoid carrying a phone and iPod – and have access to the Internet too. You can also enjoy movies on the large screen and fill in any spare time browsing the Internet.

I want to watch lots of movies – what is the best choice?

The iPod Touch or the iPhone. The iPhone is expensive if you just want to listen to music or watch movies – getting it with a phone contract is more economic, but that presupposes you want a phone too. The Touch is a more reasonably priced alternative.

How much?

What can an iPod hold? Here's a rough guide to their capacities. Why rough? Well, songs vary in length and file size, as do photo files and movies, so it's hard to give precise numbers. Take these figures as an approximation.

A 160GB iPod will hold up to:

*   40,000 songs
*   50,000 images and photos
*   200 hours of video
*   … or a combination of each.

A 80GB iPod will hold up to:

*   20,000 songs
*   25,000 images and photos
*   100 hours of video

… or a combination of each.

An 8GB iPod nano or Touch will hold up to:

*   1000 songs
*   up to 15,000 photo snapshots.

An iPod shuffle 1GB will hold up to:

*   240 songs.

Summary

Far from being a single device, the iPod is a broad family that caters for just about every need. Couple one with iTunes and you've a perfect resource for creating a fantastic music library that you can enjoy at home or on the move. If you're looking for a new one – whether you've owned one before or not – you should now be well versed in their respective merits and be able to shortlist those models most appropriate to your needs.

Like most electronic devices, your iPod is just about ready to go, straight from the box. But again like many devices, you can make the experience of owning it even better with a few well chosen accessories. In the next chapter we'll take a look at some of those on offer.

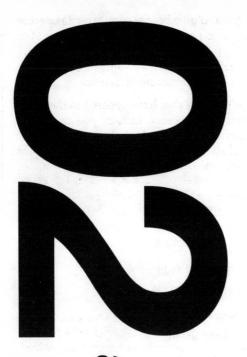

02

accessories

In this chapter you will learn:
- about the essential kit for your iPod
- about the cases and docks
- how to extend your listening experience
- about some of the iPod's eclectic accessories

Once you've acquired your iPod, the chances are that you're going to want to make the experience of ownership better. Far from being simply a device for enjoying your music on the move, it can quickly become the hub of a music (and, if your player supports it, photo and video) entertainment system.

Supporting this is a huge industry that has appeared in the wake of the success of the iPod and its peers. In fact, you can do so much with iPods that they have spawned a huge industry in accessories, perfectly matched to your player. There's no doubt that these can extend your enjoyment in many ways – some of which you may not have even considered – but it's important to be wary. Before you spend your hard-earned cash (and often large amounts of it) you need to be circumspect about what's on offer. In this chapter we'll take a look at the good, the bad and the downright ugly of iPod accessories.

Cases, skins and covers

Perhaps the first investment that anyone makes is a case. That's not surprising. The not inconsequential cost of your iPod means it makes good sense to afford it the best in protection. In fact, cases have more of a role to play than mere protection. When your iPod has a somewhat neutral – even anonymous in some cases – design, a case is the perfect way to personalize it and make your own mark.

The range of cases is truly immense and constantly changing but you'll find they all fall into distinct types:

• **Cases and bags:** the more traditional slip-in, flip-open and close and slot-in types. These generally provide the highest level of protection.

• **Skins:** close fitting, and usually made of silicon; offer good cosmetic protection and reasonably good physical protection.

• **Covers:** simple covers provide good cosmetic protection but less physical protection from damage.

Cases and bags

This is the most comprehensive group, in both styles and types. Bags include the small, pouch type that were originally designed for compact cameras and provide a very high level of protection. They come with shoulder straps, hand/wrist straps or belt clips for secure attachment to the user. Reinforcements ensure that, under normal use, the bags will protect your device from damage when dropped but the obvious drawback is that to operate the device you will need to remove it from the bag – not always convenient. Some bags are larger and also allow storage of headphones or earphones.

Cases include all those that are not figure hugging in the sense that skins are. At one end of the range are the formal cases. Designed for the office and formal situations, these tend to follow the style popularized by PDA – personal digital assistant – cases of providing a secure fitting for the device itself (and offering unhindered access to the controls) with a flip over protection for when the case is in the jacket or pocket. The cover is sufficiently rigid to prevent any damage to the screen or fascia if the case receives a glancing blow.

Bags like this probably afford the best protection and provide additional storage for accessories – but are not the most compact or discrete solution.

Perhaps not surprisingly you'll also find this style has been translated into other finishes so if leather is not your style, you can get a similar case finished in suede, denim, tweed or even tapestry. Variations on this theme see cases disguised as compact purses.

Designer case: you can have a case for your iPod Touch or iPhone that matches your favourite tartan or tweed design.

If these represent the traditional end of the market, perhaps for those that don't want to make too overt a statement about their love of technology, polycarbonate cases accentuate the contents.

The reason for using polycarbonate is that it's extremely tough and perfectly transparent: you can enjoy the clean lines of your iPod, see the (delicate) screen clearly and operate the controls unhindered. The drawback, if there is one, is that polycarbonate is almost too tough: drop an iPod cased in polycarbonate and it will be well protected from any surface damage but there's a slight risk that the shock of the impact will be passed on to the player itself.

Griffin Centerstage: this polycarbonate case from Griffin combines the ruggedness of polycarbonate with an aluminium cover that flips over to provide a convenient table stand.

Skins

Unlike cases and bags which, even in their most svelte form add some bulk to the player, skins are, as the name might suggest, skin tight, adding only millimetres to the dimensions.

Skins are generally made out of silicone – giving them a soft feel and high resistance to damage. The only downside is that their tight form-fitting style can make them hard to get on or off. However, most allow access to the dock for charging and connection to your computer without having to be removed. Those made from stretchy neoprene – the same material used for wet suits – are easier to put on and take off.

Silicone skins are available in a wide range of translucent colours and some are embellished with patterns and artwork too.

Covers

Including anything from slip-in cases to iPod socks (short, knitted socks custom-made for the iPod), jackets are probably the most informal of cover. They are also (in general) the cheapest.

Think of these more in the manner of fashion statements than high protection. They will offer some protection (especially against cosmetic damage) but rarely offer anything more than cursory protection against impact damage.

A sports jacket for your iPod

Since the earliest days, iPods have been touted as the perfect companion to people on the move – and especially for runners and joggers. Music can make a fantastic difference to those spending long hours pounding the streets or working out in the gym.

Though robust, if you want to use your device during physical exertion you need to make sure that you choose a case or jacket that does not leave it flapping around or impeding your progress. For the more active there is a sports jacket – a strong jacket that you can strap to your arm, waist or wrist.

Take care. These jackets are designed to provide resistance to the jolts and jostling of workouts – they may not offer the best impact resistance and are likely to be water resistant, rather than waterproof.

Tadpole cases

Young children, wanting to ape their elder siblings and parents, now put iPods on their wish lists, and many are successful. But how do you ensure that, in little hands, the device is going to survive the rigours of everyday life? One answer is the Tadpole case.

Tadpole Cover: ideal for young hands – and exceptionally robust – the Tadpole cover is designed to be especially rugged.

Designed by ifrogz, this is more than a simple case: it provides large grip handles to hold and carry the player and has a resilient body – more than sufficient to stand up to all the knocks and blows it's likely to be subjected to. Despite this armoured protection, access to the click wheel and the other controls is not impaired and the screen remains visible, protected behind an optional plastic overlay.

Simple protection

Of course, you don't have to choose any of these cases, skins or covers. Many people are quite happy leaving their player naked. But, as some have found, being too blasé about protection can leave your device looking a little tired. Time can take its toll. However, you can take some steps to ensure longevity.

* **Screen protection:** The weak point of most players is the screen. Screen protectors provide an almost invisible cover for the screen that, despite a diminutive thickness, makes the screen much more durable. When the protector does get scratched or damaged then you simply peel it off and apply a new one.

Screen protectors: simple covers for the screen are invisible but improve resilience.

* **Bodywork protection:** Drop your player and it's the corners and edges that are likely to take the brunt of any impact. An elasticated strip around the device adds little to its bulk but substantially to the protection. Some of these even feature a thin back to protect the back of your player.

Edge protection: soft protectors for the edge and back of your player don't compromise the looks but provide added resistance to damage.

Buying advice: cases, skins and covers

Generally speaking, cases and other covers provide protection and a degree of security. Even if you keep your player concealed, a cover of some type will prevent damage in your pocket or purse. Buy something suitable to your needs and lifestyle – bearing in mind designer-style prices reflect the label not the security or robustness. If you are more prone to dropping your player, a case will pay for itself in no time!

Docks

Your iPod (and here we're talking about all iPods except the shuffle) needs a dock: it provides the essential connection to your computer in order to synchronize and transfer data. That dock may be the desktop version – a slot-in type that displays your device to best advantage and lets you conveniently operate the controls, or it may be a compact one – a simple cable terminating in a dock connector.

Whatever dock you have, the chances are that the aftermarket accessory versions will offer extra functionality and control. This might include enhanced connectivity (to televisions and video devices for example), more effective remote control or something more portable.

The universal dock

Back in the early days of iPods you would get a dock included in the package. Now you need to spend (an admittedly modest amount) to acquire one as an accessory. The good news is that the universal dock that you'll get is compatible with just about all iPods made to date (so it could be a good move to upgrade your old dock, if you have one), and should be compatible with those to come. All you need do is insert the adaptor into the dock that corresponds with your particular model.

This dock also features remote control for the iPod (though the simple remote control needs to be bought separately) allowing you to access some simple control features. As such it's not quite as comprehensive as some alternatives on the market.

Full remote control docks

The likes of Griffin, Kensington and Keyspan have been quick to supply an eager market with iPod accessories. For docking your device, they offer the TuneCenter, Entertainment Dock and AV Dock respectively, all of which offer extended functionality compared with the Universal dock. Typically, this extended activity enables more comprehensive control of the player by means of better remote control features.

You'll also find that all docks now offer connectivity with video systems so that you can connect your iPod to a TV – to replay any video content you may have downloaded. If you are using an older model that does not have any video or photo capabilities you can ignore these connections and features – until you upgrade.

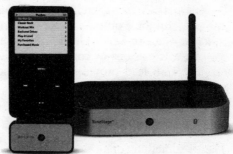

Belkin Tunestage: a wireless
solution for iPod docking.

Enhanced remote control

The remote control features offered via many of the docks discussed here will seem limited, to those used to the functionality of the remote controls provided, for example, with your TV or audio system. However, some remotes offer substantially enhanced features. Consider Keyspan's TuneView remote. This can be partnered with the AV dock and used in place of the more rudimentary remote

TuneView remote: offering enhanced functionality, including
a colour info screen, the TuneView remote allows you to charge
your iPod whilst replaying your choice of music.

normally supplied. Using RF to communicate with the dock (giving the potential for room-to-room rather than same-room control provided by infra red) this remote displays – in full colour – details of your music collection and will allow you to navigate your music library and the playlists stored in the iPod as well as giving you normal control functions.

Pocket docks

When you are on the move you probably won't be too concerned with full-function, full-sized remote controls. And you probably could do without the need to carry a full-sized dock around when you want to synchronize your music library. For these occasions you can equip yourself with a pocket dock. Suitable for the smallest of pockets, these (such as the appropriately named PocketDock AV from SendStation) feature a dock connector at one end, and three outputs on the other: a minijack output, USB connector and an S-video lead. The latter is designed to link the iPod with televisions or computer monitors, with an S connector. The USB lead provides for the syncing and recharging of your iPod.

Wireless docking solutions

There's something of an elegant solution we're overlooking here. How about using the iPod itself as a remote? It's got a terrific interface that's easy to use with one hand (even in the dark) and using this would save investing in a second remote control that needs to copy much of the functionality. That's the rationale behind kit like Belkin's TuneStage and Logitech's Wireless Music System. Both these use Bluetooth (the same communications system you might find in wireless computer keyboards and mice or between a mobile phone and a wireless earpiece) to transmit your music selections to an audio system.

The kit comprises a small module that you attach to the iPod and a receiver box that attaches to the audio system – simple and elegant. Of course, as you are using your iPod disconnected you will need to keep it charged periodically – perhaps using a conventional dock.

Buying advice: docks

There's no doubt that a dock offers great convenience for charging and syncing your iPod – whether the extra features, such as TV connectivity are worth the additional cost will depend upon your use. If you plan to use your iPod for music and audio they are clearly superfluous; if you download videos and movies, essential.

02

Earphones and headphones

You can spend significant amounts of money on your iPod. Unfortunately this expensive hardware is then connected to a very cheap pair of earphones. The result is mediocre sound quality. Sadly, few of us realize how mediocre until we have the opportunity to compare the sound quality with something more effective. So, if you recognize you need something better, what are your options?

Earphones

Your iPod normally comes with ordinary earphones. These are generally of average quality, but you can get some that are substantially more effective. The drawback with all of these types is that some people don't like something sitting in their ears and others have problems with them falling out, particularly under physical exertion such as running or gym work. For those people there are some designs that feature an earclip. This lets you accurately place the earpiece over, rather than in, the ear.

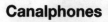

Earphones with earclips: this design allows the earphone itself to be positioned exactly over – but not in – the entrance to the ear canal.

Canalphones

Sometimes considered a specialized form of earphones, these need to be inserted into the ear canal. That makes them less likely to fall out but also more uncomfortable for some to use. The pay-off is that the sound is more precisely focused and directed at the eardrum. An acoustically well-designed pair of canalphones will offer better sound quality compared to standard earphones. Also, because they fill the ear canal they are effective at excluding extraneous sound.

Notionally like earphones, canalphones are inserted in the ear canal to ensure focused sound.

Headphones

The benefit of earphones and canalphones is that they are light-weight and discrete. Headphones are heavier, larger and are less likely to be comfortable for longer listening sessions. However, the larger size allows for larger speaker enclosures that can produce better sound.

Though providing the best sound, headphones can be tiring to wear for extended periods.

The manufacturers of headphones have long appreciated the virtues of this larger speaker geometry but have also realized that few of us would be willing to wander the streets, get on trains and buses or even drive our car wearing such a pair. And there were those who did not want their hair messed up in the interests of good sound. Hence, spurred on by the burgeoning iPod market, headphone designers have come up with interesting hybrid designs.

So watch out for:

◆ **Sports bands:** headphones that sit at the back of the head rather than on the top.

Sports bands sit around the top of the neck and provide a more convenient and less fatiguing way to support your headphone speakers.

- **Foldups:** headphones whose headband folds away for stowage and are reasonably discrete when worn.

- **Earclips:** headphone style speaker assemblies that don't have a band connecting them at all; instead a clip goes over the ear to hold them in place, rather like those used with some earphones.

Noise cancelling

A design that has become increasingly popular and affordable in recent times is the noise cancelling system. Available as both headphones and canalphones, these provide the ultimate in listening: the headphones monitor the ambient sound and produce a signal that cancels this out, so that, with no music playing though them, the result would be near silence. That allows you to enjoy your music as if in silent surroundings.

Some of these designs are somewhat cumbersome – they include an extra module that's essentially a microphone for picking up the ambient noise – and feature quite substantial ear sections to ensure that as much sound is excluded in the first place. However, as the technology improves and becomes more compact, smaller models (including canalphones) are appearing.

Noise cancelling headphones: looking similar to conventional headphones, noise cancelling models provide great listening conditions, particularly when travelling or in noisy environments.

Cordless and wireless

Cordless headphones have been around for some time and have offered reasonably good quality sound reproduction when paired up with a home hifi system. Unfortunately, these require a moderately large receiver unit that needs to be connected to the hifi itself and, as such, does not lend itself to cordless music reproduction on the move.

More recently we've seen the arrival of more compact systems based on the Bluetooth communications technology. This was born from the cordless headsets designed for use with mobile phones. Both conventional headphones and earphones featuring cordless Bluetooth technology are available. Both are slightly more bulky than corded versions as they need to accommodate the extra communications technology and also because they need to carry their own power, in the form of batteries.

Watching iPod video on the move

Use your iPod video for movies and video? With a good pair of headphones you'll be able to enjoy the sound of the programming but you'll still be watching on a small screen. Use a video headset and you can transform your viewing from the small screen to a mega-large one, albeit a virtual one. Video headsets use optical systems coupled with small, high-resolution LCD TV panels to give the wearer the impression that they are watching a large screen from a modest distance. Much more restful on the eyes and remarkably effective. The drawback is that, coupled with good headphones they can leave you divorced from your surroundings.

Video headsets: ideal for keeping the children quiet on long journeys.

iPod speakers and hifi connectivity

From their inception, iPods were designed to be personal. They are the spiritual heirs to the tape and CD-based Walkmans of the 1980s and 1990s. However, it was quickly realized that the compromises in sound quality brought about by compressing music to fit the players was not significant and players could provide a source of music to be shared. Suddenly it appeared that these devices could take on all forms of music player. So now you can enhance your iPod to provide background music in your office through to enhancing the capabilities of your home hifi system. Here's how your iPod can grow with you.

Foldaway speakers

You might imagine that a speaker little larger than a typical player would be hard pressed to deliver good quality sound of any sort, let alone good stereo. You may be pleased to know that you are wrong. Taking advantage of the advanced speaker technology that makes the diminutive elements of earphones so potent, mini fold-away speakers can deliver sound quality that defies their scale and are quite sufficient to provide good quality sound for a modest sized room. Don't expect deep booming bass or success-fully reproduced high volumes but as a replacement for a small tape or CD player, you'll be pleasantly surprised. Better still, foldaway designs let you pack the speakers into a small bag to follow you on your travels or holidays. Depending on the model you may find you've a dock and a minijack cable socket to allow any other device to be attached.

This folding speaker unfolds to reveal a dock.

Compact speakers

If you are willing to compromise slightly on portability – and we are only talking slightly – you can go for speakers that are a bit bigger and can give some added volume and punch to your sound. At this size you're likely to find an iPod dock as standard though you'll also get the connector for any other player. Some designs have interchangeable dock units that allow other play-ers to be connected directly.

In this category you can also find the digital music version of the clock radio. Combine a music player dock, radio, clock and great speakers (albeit in a compact form) and you've a great multipurpose music player that will even wake you in the morning to the sounds of your favourite tracks.

iPod meets clock radio. This speaker system combines an iPod dock with a clock radio and remarkably good speakers.

Portable speakers

Still larger – but remaining portable – these speakers are sufficient to fill a medium to large-sized domestic room with good quality sound. The extra size of the speakers will mean not only that you can get a good volume without distortion but also that you'll begin to get some of that powerful bass that will start filling out your sound. Many of these units are designed to be the modern equivalent of the ghetto blaster – though much more tastefully styled and using the music player rather than CD as the principal sound source.

This compact portable speaker can be supplied with a complementary carry bag.

Bigger speakers

Once an amplifier was obligatory for most sound systems. You needed this component to take the signal from your tape, LP or CD and amplify it sufficiently to feed the speakers with a chosen volume. Speaker technology has moved on and many speakers today feature active technology. That means the amplification is built into the speakers themselves. So you can plug in a source – such as an iPod – and have full control over the volume without any additional components.

Active speakers, in the middle range in terms of quality and price are capable of delivering exceptional quality and this has not been lost on manufacturers who have successfully incorporated them into music player systems. With just a docking unit and speakers they can be very discrete (depending, of course, on the speaker design) but capable of very high quality sound. Throw in a sub woofer and you have the perfect sound system – with even the bass well filled.

Mini hifi

Mini hifi systems have been popular for some time, usurping the big, bland, black boxes popular in the early 1990s. They feature a central module for all the sound sources and speakers that can be placed at will around the room. But with the simple inclusion of a dock (and often the removal of tape and CD elements) the mini hifi has been reborn.

The full hifi

Already got a great hifi? Connect your music player direct (use the auxiliary input if you don't have a dedicated input) via an appropriate cable (available from your local electronics store) and breathe new life into it. Add in a dock to make sure that you keep the player charged during those long party sessions.

You can go fully wireless with your music collection – we'll have more to say about this in Chapter 5.

High end sound: no discussion on sound systems could be complete without this. It's a top of the market valve amp, perfectly matched to iPods. It looks good and sounds good too!

More accessories

Browse any online or bricks-and-mortar stores specializing in digital music accessories and you'll see that cases, docks and hifi accessories are just the beginning. There's an awful lot more there trying to attract your attention. Let's take a select look at some.

Power and charging

Whatever music player you have chosen, you can enjoy it only so long as the power lasts. Fortunately, in day-to-day use the power from the onboard batteries will last surprisingly long but for longer sessions, or if you choose to watch video or share photos, the battery life can drop dramatically.

You can charge your iPod every time you connect to a computer but there will be times you won't be able to. In these cases it makes sense to have an alternative. There are chargers that will operate when you are in the car, connect straight to mains electricity and even use solar power to top up your batteries.

You can even get auxiliary battery packs that attach to your player and extend the life of the main battery pack.

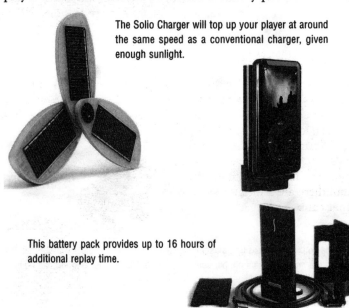

The Solio Charger will top up your player at around the same speed as a conventional charger, given enough sunlight.

This battery pack provides up to 16 hours of additional replay time.

Car adaptors

As well as competing with domestic sound systems, the iPod has managed to evict the tape and CD from many car interiors. A number of models now come with a connector for an iPod and, depending on the installation, you can even control the device using the standard car hifi controls. We'll look at some of these in more detail later.

Microphones

Want to use your player as a voice recorder too? Then you need a microphone module. These devices also include the software to integrate with the host device and then allow the controls to be used for recording. Don't expect the highest quality sound recording direct through these micro-phones, but for note-taking they are ideal.

Griffin's iTalk pro offers good quality sound recording from your iPod.

The wild and wacky

Okay, so they won't improve your sound quality, or offer enhanced performance but there are some things in the accessory catalogues that just defy categorization. One such, shown here is the iDog. A friend of the iFish and iCat, it will dance to the music from your player and you can even interact with it. Fun – and there are a lot more where that came from.

iDog: the perfect companion to your iPod?

Summary

Accessories? Some are more or less essential. Think of cases – you will need one to afford your device protection from dramatic falls and day-to-day wear. Others are less than essential but useful – we can put docks in this category. There's no doubt a simple dock is useful but not essential: you can charge and synchronize with a basic cable. More sophisticated docks provide functionality that, depending on your needs, may be crucial for connecting, for example, to a TV.

Additional speakers are all about extending the capabilities of your device, as are car adaptors, microphones and many other devices that we don't have the space for here. The chances are, like most of us, you'll be drawn to many of them. But think twice before you buy so that you only end up with those great accessories that you'll actually enjoy and use.

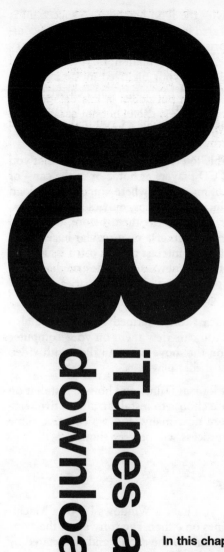

03

iTunes and downloads

In this chapter you will learn:
- about iTunes
- how to install iTunes
- about the features found in iTunes
- about digital music services
- some of the differences between different digital music services

One of the key reasons why the iPod has been so successful is that it is completely integrated into iTunes – a neat piece of computer software that comprises the digital media player's library and music store. It is here, in iTunes' main library, that you can keep all your digital music and your digitized music including those tracks from your old vinyl LPs, singles and cassettes that you've converted into digital form. We'll discover how do to this later. This is also where any purchases you make from the iTunes Store will be copied.

It's also where you'll be able to create your own CDs – that you can play on conventional CD players at home or in the car – of your favourite selections of music and where you can download (and store) other media, including videos, movies and podcasts. Podcasts, if you've never come across them before, are audio recordings that you can elect to receive on a regular basis. They may be on any subject – special interest groups often issue their own podcasts – or can feature news summaries or digests of radio broadcasts. Podcasts are often issued as a series and new episodes, when available, can be automatically downloaded.

Video versions of the podcast (often termed vodcasts) are also available for download. You can view them on your computer (from within iTunes) or on the move using an iPod with video capabilities or some other media player.

We will now take a closer look at iTunes and how to install it on your computer. Should you choose to install an alternative service too (of which there are now many, and we examine some later in this chapter) the process will be very similar.

Installing iTunes

It doesn't matter whether you have a Windows PC or a Macintosh – you can install iTunes on either. The software is the same on both, differing only in some of the details and as dictated by the differences between each computer's operating system.

Installing on a Macintosh computer

iTunes comes preinstalled on all new Macintosh computers and will be available for use as soon as you get your computer up and running for the first time. It's also available as part of a raft of the iLife applications. You need to do nothing more than click on the iTunes logo that appears in the dock.

If, for some reason, you don't have iTunes on your Macintosh you can get a copy from the Apple website: **www.apple.com/ itunes,** and install it following the method described below for the Windows version (though obviously selecting the Macintosh version).

Macintosh users can start iTunes by clicking on the icon in the dock.

Installing iTunes on a Windows computer

If you own a Windows computer you can still get iTunes for free, though this time it isn't installed as standard. Visit **www.apple.com/itunes** and click the **Download iTunes** button.

Click on the Download iTunes button to begin downloading iTunes to your computer.

Choose the version of iTunes that's compatible with your system. You'll need to give your email address to begin the download – select, or deselect the adjacent buttons if you want (or don't want) news from iTunes and the iTunes Store sent to that address.

The Download now pane allows you to select the relevant version for your operating system.

The download will now begin and will take just a few minutes.

You can also install iTunes from the disc that accompanies some iPod models. Though this method is okay (and essential if you don't have an Internet connection), the chances are that you'll be able to get a more up-to-date version by downloading it directly from the Apple website.

Updating your version of iTunes

Apple is continually making iTunes better. As users, we see the fruits of their labours in the form of version updates. Sometimes these make the functionality better, sometimes they fix problems (no software today can be totally bug-free) and sometimes they add new features. Minor, incremental upgrades are indicated by a discrete change in the version number: for example when version 7.1 was upgraded to 7.2. Even more minor changes may be indicated thus: version 7.1.1 to 7.1.2.

Some updates are more significant – such as when a major new feature like the Store was added. These are usually indicated by a change in the main number of iTunes – as, in the past, from iTunes 5 to iTunes 6. Because any update should make your version of iTunes more stable and often offer greater functionality, you should upgrade whenever new versions become available. How do you know a new version is available? Apple provide a Software Updater that will advise you that new software is available and ask you whether you'd like to install it. The updater will appear automatically soon after an update is announced and is available for downloading.

Starting iTunes

You can start iTunes in different ways:

* **Windows users** can click on the iTunes shortcut on the desktop (you can choose to add a shortcut to the desktop as part of the installation process), or select **Start > Programs > Apple > iTunes**.

* **Mac users** can select **iTunes** from the dock.

With either platform you'll find that iTunes will normally open – if it is not already open – when you connect your iPod. It may also open (depending on your computer's settings) when you insert a CD into the CD drive. Why? Because iTunes is pre-empting you, making an inspired guess that if you are inserting a CD you might want to play the music on it.

You can use the iTunes preference settings (of which more later) to adjust these settings to allow iTunes to automatically play a CD, or import the music tracks on it.

When you install iTunes for the first time you'll be prompted to complete the installation – nothing very complex – by agreeing to the (inevitable and tediously long to read) licence agreement. You may also be prompted on whether you want iTunes to trawl its way through your computer to find any music files scattered over the hard disc.

A tour of the iTunes interface

Once the installation is complete you'll see the main iTunes window, the interface, as shown here. Don't worry if yours doesn't look quite like this. Upgrades can bring new features and a modified look, and there are detail differences between the Windows and Macintosh versions.

Here's an overview of the key components. Don't worry either about the details – we'll be exploring each of these features later.

The main iTunes Window.

1 **Sources panel:** these are all the sources of music (and other media) that you have access to. The layout and amount of

information in this pane will change according to the extent of your music collection and any music devices you may have.

2 **Library options:** click on Music here to see a listing of the music that you can replay via iTunes. Other resources – such as TV shows, podcasts and even audio books have their own options to make selection simpler. You can also access games (for downloading to your iPod) and radio stations too. Did you realize that iTunes provides access to hundreds of radio stations too? We'll discover more later!

3 **iTunes Store:** here's where you can access the iTunes Music Store when you want to purchase additional music, videos or movies. You can download free content (such as podcasts here too).

4 **Connected/installed devices:** when your iPod is connected, it will appear here – ready to have content added, should you wish. If you have a CD loaded, you'll find that displayed here too.

5 **Playlists:** your music library can become large very quickly. It's unlikely that you'd want to play it all from the beginning or in the sequence that they are stored in the library so iTunes lets you create playlists – customized lists of songs. You might choose to keep individual music albums in a playlist, or create your own thematic collections – blues, jazz or electronica, for example.

6 **Library listing:** select your music library (or one of the alternatives) and the contents of that library are shown here. You can alter the display by selecting one of the buttons (see item 10).

7 **Now Playing:** you can see the track playing and monitor its progress in this area. There are some hidden features here that we'll explore soon.

8 **Play controls:** to play, pause, rewind or fast-forward through your music, use these controls. They are exactly the same as you might find on a CD player or tape recorder. You can also move forward or back through a track by dragging the little diamond shown in the **Now Playing** window.

9 **Search:** as your collection grows, finding a specific track can take longer and longer. Enter the name in this search window and it'll appear in the main **Library** listing window. You can

also search by using the first few characters of the name or, say, the band. When you select Music Store in this window it lets you search the whole Store in exactly the same way.

10 **Display type:** the library listing window shown here gives you all the essential information about your library tracks. Click on the other buttons here and you'll see a pictorial display or an album-based version.

11 **Shortcut buttons:** these shortcut buttons let you shuffle the music played and open the Artwork pane or add a playlist.

12 **Artwork:** when you download music from the Music Store you'll find the cover art of the track or album will appear automatically here. If you've downloaded music from a CD you can let iTunes grab artwork from the Internet.

You may also have additional controls if you choose to share your music collection with other computers, or other users share their collections with you. In this case, you'll see a shared libraries option appear in the Sources panel.

Going large, going small

There's an awful lot of information to present in a single window with iTunes. You may want to make the window larger – to see more information at a time – or smaller if you want music just playing in the background and don't want the full window taking up valuable screen space.

* Like most windows on your computer screen you can drag the corner of the iTunes window to make it larger. You can also drag the edges of panes within the window to make them larger or smaller.

* To shrink the window down so that it only displays the **Now Playing** window and the playback controls press **[Control]** + **[M]**, or on a Macintosh, press the green button.

The main controls.

* If that's not small enough you can also lose the **Now Playing** window by dragging the corner inwards with your mouse.

The essential controls.

* Whichever format you use, you'll always have access to the playback controls and a volume slider, just in case you need to turn the sound down when the phone rings!

* You can also minimize the open iTunes window to the taskbar (Windows) or dock (Macintosh) by clicking on the appropriate button in the title bar.

The iTunes Store

Before we take a closer look at some of the features in the iTunes window, let's take a look at just one feature – the iTunes Store. Let's make it clear here that the iTunes Store is by no means the only way, or the only place, that you can purchase digital music. But by virtue of it being just a single mouse click from the main iTunes window it certainly scores on accessibility.

The home page of the iTunes Store.

To get your first look, click on the iTunes Store button. Using the Store does need an Internet connection – if you are offline you won't be able to gain access. Assuming you do have an Internet connection (and the Store is optimized for broadband) you'll soon see the front window of the Store. It'll probably look nothing like that shown here – testament to the frequency that music and other content is updated.

Don't let its overtly commercial appearance worry you. You won't inadvertently purchase the entire back catalogue of EMI through a couple of accidental mouse clicks – buying music requires a little more effort!

Promotions like Single of the Week draw your attention to new and interesting material.

There's more on purchasing music from the iTunes Store – and acquiring music generally – in the next chapter.

The iTunes Wifi Music Store

Announced along with the iPod Touch, the Wifi Music Store lets owners of this iPod – and of iPhones – search, browse, preview, purchase and download music tracks and albums by connecting their device to a WiFi network. Music downloaded is then synced with the owner's main iTunes library next time the iPod syncs. The WiFi store is in virtually all respects similar to the 'full' store and, although there are minor operational differences dictated by the device, anyone familiar with the computer-based version will quickly find their way around the mobile edition.

More features of iTunes

As you get more familiar with iTunes you'll soon discover it offers a very logical and clear layout and you'll soon be clicking your way around your music collection.

Here are a couple of additional features that we've mentioned in passing but deserve a second mention.

Radio in iTunes: the Radio button in the Sources pane provides access to a huge number of radio stations. These are stations that, as well as broadcasting conventionally through transmitters and direct to radio sets also stream (that is, transmit in real time) over the Internet. There are also some that don't strictly qualify as radio stations because they only transmit on the Net.

iTunes divides the available stations into genres and often provides radio stations with different bit rates. Bit rates? This is a measure of the amount of data transmitted per second. As you might guess, the higher the bit rate, the greater the amount of data transmitted per second, the better the signal and the better the sound reproduction. Bigger numbers are better! The same rules apply to music downloaded to iTunes and video downloads as well.

Purchased Music: once you start purchasing music from the Store, you can keep an eye on your purchases by clicking here. You'll see all your purchased music and this will make it easier to back up your collection. It's important that you back up (that is, make a copy of these music tracks) in case something happens to your computer or its hard disc. Once you've purchased music you become responsible for copies so it makes sense to copy them to a CD or another computer drive periodically. Then, if the worst happens, you can copy the tracks from your backup onto your new, or repaired, computer.

Subscriptions vs. Pay Per Track

Before taking a look at some of the alternatives to iTunes, it's worth taking a modest diversion to examine some of the ways you can purchase your chosen tracks – and the ways that the music companies restrict your subsequent use of that music.

Services differ in the way that you pay for the music. The basic iTunes model is simple. You pay a fixed price for a track, and a fairly fixed price for an album. iTunes does offer two prices for some single tracks – the standard price offers good quality but includes digital management rights coding. This is a special, inaudible code buried in the music that prevents it being played freely on multiple devices or on devices other than iPods. For a premium price you can purchase a higher quality copy (they boast a higher bit rate) without the digital management rights coding. This, it should be added, doesn't mean you are free to use and share the tracks as you wish – the same copyright rules apply – but you can, for example, play it on devices and over networks that don't normally allow protected tracks to be played.

Some services offer subscription-based access instead. Pay a single monthly fee and you have access to a fixed number of tracks or, depending on the service (and subscription) the entire store's catalogue. Again depending on the service, tracks that are downloaded may be retained when you discontinue your subscription or will expire (not be playable) when the subscription expires.

Which is best? It depends on you. If you like ownership of music, the pay-per-track model is probably best. If you like access to a large amount of music and have evolving tastes, a subscription may be better.

More music download sites

There's no doubt that the clarity of design and ease of use have deservedly given iTunes its pre-eminent position. But there are a number of other sources out there that offer similar services and music stores. If your favourite music can't be found in the iTunes Store you might well find it on another.

Here's a rundown of some of the more popular digital music stores.

eMusic (eMusic.com): a subscription-based service that allows music to be downloaded free of any restrictions. You can, then, burn your selections to CD and won't find your selections disappearing if you subsequently choose to end your subscription. Because there is no digital rights management included, tracks from the big four record labels are not currently available through this service.

Virgin Digital (virgindigital.com): a similar service to iTunes Music Store from a major label. One useful feature is Music Insurance – should you lose your music collection as downloaded you can download all your purchased tracks for free again.

Napster (napster.co.uk, napster.com): a service that offers downloading by pay-per-track or two subscription options. Anyone that might have been involved with digital music for some time might recognize the name – Napster was also the name for an illegal music sharing system (that circumvented all copyrighting) but be assured, this system is 100% legal.

Napster is a popular music library and download service.

Boutique Stores: these stores look after the discerning ears of the music specialist and often list tracks in genres that are poorly served by the mainstream services.

There are also stores that allow musicians to upload their own music tracks for wider distribution and sale. Examples include Amie Street, which uses a complex (but automated) process to price tracks according to their popularity. If you upload one of your tracks and it proves a hit, you'll find its price per download increases, its visibility rises and your income will too.

Note that some music stores will only work on Windows PCs. You should also check that your favourite digital music store will download tracks that are compatible with your iPod or digital music player – again not all are.

Summary

After reading this chapter you should be aware of what your iPod and iTunes can offer and have a feel for how simple they are to use – also, how simple it is to install one of these applications on your computer should you not have one installed already.

Of course, what we have seen so far of iTunes is just a shell, a place where we can safely deposit our music (and other) tracks. Next it's time to look at how we can start filling our digital music library, collecting together all those CDs, tapes and even old vinyl recordings.

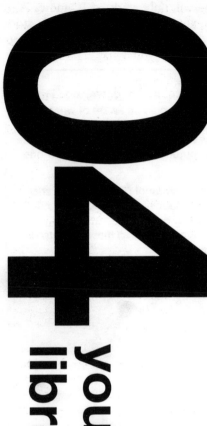

04 your iTunes library

In this chapter you will learn how to:

- add music to your digital library
- add track, artist and album information
- import tape and LP music
- buy music from the iTunes Store
- synchronize your iPod and music collection
- back up your collection

So you've installed your copy of iTunes. You now need to start filling it with the best of your music collection. Most people's music collections today are likely to be based on CDs but you may also have other recordings that you'll want to add to your new digital collection. Those may be:

- Digital music tracks you've acquired or downloaded prior to the installation of iTunes.

- Your collection, and your family's, of LPs, EPs, singles and other vinyl recordings.

- Old cassette tapes.

Before you can begin to import your music you need to identify whether your originals are digital or analogue, as the import process is slightly different for each. Usually, digital music will comprise that which you've downloaded from a website (or a music store like iTunes Store) and that recorded on CD. Other digital sources which are admittedly less common are DAT – digital audio tape – or MiniDisc. Because these are rare, and the equipment to replay them directly to a computer even rarer, we'll treat these as analogue sources, i.e. those that were recorded without using digital technology. In practice, that's vinyl and tape.

What's the difference between analogue and digital recordings? Analogue formats record audio directly as a series of audio signals written to the tape or disc, in proportion to the original music. To put it simply (perhaps too simply for the purist) a loud sound would be recorded as a wide groove engraved on a disc or large magnetized patch on tape; a quiet sound as a narrower groove. Your computer won't understand how to interpret these signals directly as they are not in a suitable form. For digital recordings the audio signal is converted into a digital code – a string of '0's and '1's – that your computer will understand. Unlike an analogue recording which can never be copied with the fidelity of the original (which is why copies of analogue recordings are always inferior) a digital signal is easily copied without any degradation.

Importing CDs to your digital music library

Before we take a look at the potentially more tricky material to copy, let's begin by examining how you can import your CD collection to iTunes.

With iTunes installed on your computer all you need to do is insert a CD and this will normally start iTunes (if it's not already running). It will immediately ask you whether you'd like to import the tracks on the CD. If you don't get this prompt, don't worry. You can activate it – so that the prompt will appear every time you insert a CD – via the **Preferences**.

1 Open the **Preferences** menu option, select **Advanced** and then choose **Importing**.

2 Select **Ask to Import CD** from the **On CD Insert** menu.

If you've a large collection of CDs to import and you'd like to save even more time you can change this menu selection to 'Import and Eject'. Then, every time you insert a CD the tracks will be imported into your iTunes library and, on completion, the CD ejected.

By changing the Preferences you can alter the way iTunes reacts when a disc is inserted. It can import immediately and then eject the CD, ask you what you'd like to do, or simply show the disc.

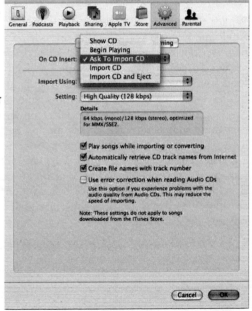

Selecting tracks to import

Though you could import the entire album in one go, there may be some where you don't want to import some of the tracks. Often you'll have an album that contains some filler tracks or ones you just don't like. In this case select 'Show CD' in the Preferences menu.

	Name	Time	Artist	Album	Genre
1	☑ Love Won't Let You Down	4:20	Swing Out Sister	Where Our Love Gr...	Pop
2	☑ Where Our Love Grows	3:55	Swing Out Sister	Where Our Love Gr...	Pop
3	☑ When The Laughter Is Over	3:42	Swing Out Sister	Where Our Love Gr...	Pop
4	☑ Certain Shades Of Limelight	4:06	Swing Out Sister	Where Our Love Gr...	Pop
5	☑ From My Window	4:42	Swing Out Sister	Where Our Love Gr...	Pop
6	☑				Pop
7	☑				Pop
8	☑	Would you like to import the CD "Where Our Love Grows" into your iTunes library?			Pop
9	☑				Pop
10	☑	☐ Do not ask me again			Pop
11	☑				Pop
12	☑		No	Yes	Pop

Select **Ask to Import** in the Preferences and you'll see this dialogue box each time you insert a CD.

Now you'll notice a small CD icon has appeared in the Sources pane of iTunes and the main window has changed to display the tracks on the CD, rather than your full library. By default all the tracks on the album will be imported: this is indicated by the little check boxes to the left of each track title. Clear the check marks of those you do not want. When you import the album these tracks will be skipped.

When the CD listing is shown, click on the check marks to exclude specific tracks from the recording. Here odd numbered ones have been excluded.

	Name
1	☐ Love Won't Let You Down
2	☑ Where Our Love Grows
3	☐ When The Laughter Is Over
4	☑ Certain Shades Of Limelight
5	☐ From My Window
6	☑ Caipirinha
7	☐ Where Our Love Grows (A Cap...
8	☑ Let The Stars Shine
9	☐ We'll Find A Place
10	☑ Happy Ending
11	☐ La Source
12	☑ Love Won't Let You Down (Mor...

CD track and album information

Did you notice, as you were considering which tracks should be imported, that the individual tracks on the CD (which would normally be listed as 'Track 1', 'Track 2') are now shown with their actual names? Also, the name of the artists and album has also appeared. This information will be stored in the library along with the music tracks, saving you a great deal of time typing in this information yourself. How did iTunes know all this disc information?

Interestingly it didn't get it from the disc itself. Instead iTunes identified the disc (using an identifier that is unique to every CD and called the 'Table of Contents') and then searched on the Internet for all the information relating to this particular disc.

Note that if your disc is still showing 'Track 1', 'Track 2' and so on you can force iTunes to look for the track names by selecting **Advanced > Get CD track Names**. The names should then be forthcoming. If they are still not found that may be because:

- ◆ The CD you're trying to import is not in the database that iTunes checks against.

- ◆ You are not connected to the Internet.

If this is the case you can manually type in the track names (and other information) and, assuming you have a connection to the Internet, send these off to the master database so that others who connect to the database can download the names. To do this select **Advanced > Send CD Track Names**.

Sometimes, when iTunes tries to display disc information it will appear confused: it will present you with two (or perhaps more) sets of information that correspond to your disc. That's because two (or more) people originally uploaded track names and used different names, spelling or even punctuation (the entire database of track information is produced by users). When this happens you'll be given the choice of which set of info to use for your disc.

The organization that operates and manages the database, Gracenote, actually does a very good job of managing and editing information so conflicts like this are actually very rare.

Importing

Once you've selected which tracks you want, you can start the process. Click on the **Import** button to download your CD tracks along with all the associated information. How long will it take?

That depends on the music, your computer and the bit rate. Remember this from the last chapter? We'll talk about it again in a moment, but the higher the bit rate the more information there is to be processed and so the longer it will take. Even so, as a good rule of thumb, the import will happen fast – between 6 and 12 times the normal speed of replaying the music. So, a 60 minute audio CD will take between five and ten minutes.

You can check progress in the main window. The display panel will show which track is being imported and how much time is remaining. It will also show the speed of importing (over 12× the replay time in this screenshot). As the tracks are imported small tick marks appear next to their number in the listing whilst the current track is shown by a disc with a wavy line running through. If it's been selected in the Preferences, the imported tracks will play (at normal speed) as the import is in progress.

Completion is signalled by an audible chord or chime.

Importing in progress: you can monitor the importing of your CD tracks – as you listen to the tracks playing in the background.

Adjusting bit rates and import settings

The bit rate, as we mentioned earlier, determines how good the sound quality of your imports will be. The greater the bit rate, the higher the quality. So higher rates are always to be preferred but there is a caveat. You will notice the increase in quality if you change the bit rate setting up to a certain point. Beyond this, our hearing is not sufficiently discerning to notice any improvement. For most people this is why iTunes (like most other digital music systems) has a default setting of around 128kbps. Increase this and you'll only increase the file size.

The trouble is, some people can still recognize the improvements offered by higher bit rates. Therefore, iTunes lets you increase the setting. To do this you need to go to the Preferences again, and select Advanced and then Importing. Use the pull-down menu to select a higher bit rate (you may need to click on the Advanced tab to do this, depending on the version of iTunes you are using).

Most people wouldn't know the difference between 128 and 180kbps, for example, as the systems used to compress the data are highly effective. The more discerning audiophile may well not want to compromise on quality so it's good to know this feature is there.

If you fall into the category of audiophile then you may also want to make use of another feature in the Importing dialogue box, Variable Bit Rate. Check this box and the importing software will modify the way it imports music. Rather than using a standard data rate, no matter what the music is, it will vary the bit rate accordingly. More complex, detailed pieces of music will be recorded at higher rates, quiet, simple pieces at a lower one.

Adding music from tapes and LPs

Adding analogue music isn't quite as simple as digital: we need to find some way to connect our analogue source – whether it's a turntable, tape player or even a radio – to the computer, and then to convert the analogue signal to digital.

Many people's first guess at this is to use an output from the analogue source – say the headphone output – and connect it to the microphone input of the computer. With the right software this would give you a result – of sorts – but not one that would deliver a high quality recording. Microphone inputs are matched to microphones – not hifi components.

Instead we need to use what audio engineers (and hifi buffs) call a line input. Some will be lucky enough to have a computer that has a line input but these, sad to say, are few and far between. You can, however, add a line input using a device such as Griffin's iMic. It's an inexpensive unit that connects to a USB socket on your computer and can then be switched to provide a line input. Connect to this and you're nearly ready to go. 'Nearly' because you'll also need some software to receive and interpret the signal coming from your iMic.

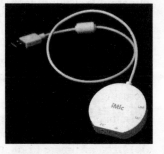

Griffin Technology's iMic gives any computer the ability to accept line level inputs – essential for digitizing analogue recordings.

You can find some software to do this on the Internet as freeware or shareware but, if you don't want to risk these applications there are some low-price commercial applications to consider.

Macintosh users might want to consider CD Spin Doctor. Despite its name, it's designed to digitize analogue audio from LPs and tapes and can let you define tracks and enhance the sound as it is recorded to, potentially, make it sound better than the original. Best of all, it uses an iTunes-style interface to make

CD Spin Doctor: this Roxio product uses an iTunes-like interface to expedite your digital recordings.

operation pretty intuitive. You can even send your digitized audio direct to iTunes.

For Windows users there is the Easy Media Creator that, like CD Spin Doctor, by Roxio, is a good choice for digitizing your analogue recordings.

Using a digitizer

You can also convert a signal (and this can include video signals too) from analogue to digital using an analogue-to-digital converter box. Also known as an A to D converter, or simply a digitizer, you connect your analogue source to one side of the box and the computer to the other. This provides a digital signal for your computer to record directly and subsequently import into iTunes.

Importing MiniDisc, DCC or DAT tapes

Some digital formats aren't so easy to import directly because the hardware is either no longer made or is not easily available. These formats, including MiniDisc, digital audio tape (DAT) and digital compact cassette (DCC) need to be treated as analogue sources, connecting the respective hardware to the computer via a line input (such as iMic). You would achieve a slightly higher quality were you able to copy digitally, but even via an analogue connection the results from these formats will be very good.

Adding music from the iTunes Store

One of the most exciting things about using iTunes is that it gives you simple access to the iTunes Store. Suddenly, you have instant access to millions (yes, millions) of tracks. Not only music tracks but also music videos, podcasts, audiobooks, TV programmes and even movies.

So, what are the benefits of the Store? For some it's the access – you can preview, audition and purchase any of the tracks on the store. That's ideal when you want a really hard-to-find track, or a single track that's almost impossible to get hold of otherwise. And, rather than buying a whole album, you can choose just the tracks you like.

For others it's the immediacy – you don't have to pay a visit to your local music store or order on line, you can get that latest album on the day of release and begin enjoying it in minutes.

Some visitors also use it as a music resource. As well as being able to download music from your favourite artists you'll also find a huge amount of information about them, including biographies and discographies.

Getting to the Store

To get to the Store you need only click on the iTunes Store icon in the source list. You will, of course need an Internet connection to get into, and download from, the Store.

iTunes Store: click on the icon to access the store. The button below, Purchased, will show you all the tracks you've purchased.

When the Store's home page opens it can be a bit daunting: there's a lot of information there – including details of the latest releases, top songs (in terms of downloads) along with additional info, movies and videos. (Do note that some content is only available in certain countries.)

Start your tour by taking a look at the options in the iTunes Store window. Here you can go directly to the store departments for music, movies, TV shows, audiobooks and so on. In the centre of the window are all the highlights from the Store, including any special offers, announcements and news. Towards the bottom of the screen are the 'Just for You' choices. As you buy more and more iTunes will analyse your purchases and make suggestions based on these. If you frequent Amazon, you may have taken a look at the recommendations page. Just for You works on the same principle.

The right-hand side of the page has quick links – go here if you want to change your account settings, need support or just more information.

Above this pane is the Search iTunes Store window. This is the same window that, when you are using your main library, you would use to search for a specific track. Now you can use it to find any track amongst the millions on offer.

The iTunes Store main screen.

You can browse the Store at your leisure and, if you find something that grabs your attention (or you are deliberately looking for a specific track) you can play a short 30 second audio clip to confirm you've found the right one. That's an important feature because the Store is so extensive that there are often several different versions of many tracks – you'll want to be sure you've got the right one before buying. There are no refunds for mistakes!

You'll also see that you can browse the Store in several ways. By genre, for example, as well as title or band. When you find the track – or the band – that you want you'll also find a lot more information, such as the background on the band, the top purchases for that band and the bands (or tracks) that other people who purchased the music you're auditioning also downloaded. This is a great way to check out similar music even if you've limited experience of these other bands and singers.

Buying music ...

...or for that matter, anything that's in the Store. To buy a track, or tracks, simply click on the 'Buy' buttons – Buy song or Buy album. The first time you do this you'll be prompted to create an account. All purchases are made against your account.

You can create an account either by clicking on a Buy button or from the Account option in the Quick Links box. From this select **Create New Account** and complete all the requested details. You'll be asked to:

* Agree to the terms and conditions
* Supply personal, address and security information
* Supply a credit or debit card number, or specify a PayPal account number and the address registered to the payment method.

If you've ever bought something from the Apple Store (such as hardware or software, peripherals or even books) you can shortcut this process by simply entering your Apple ID (normally your e-mail address) and the password for the Apple Store. The same information is valid for the Music Store.

You need do this only once – on future visits you need only sign in – but do remember your Apple ID and password. For your security you will need to use them when signing in and sometimes periodically thereafter.

Should you change your credit card details, or otherwise need to change the information you supplied when setting up your account you can do so when logging in, or via the Quick Link options. Click on **Account Info** and edit the information.

Login screen: from here you can create a new account or log in to an existing one.

Now, with your account configured you can proceed with your music purchases. Each time you click on a Buy button, your choice will be logged and your account debited. Unless you choose to skip it (by checking the button 'Do not display this box again') you will get a warning screen that will ask you to confirm your purchase. It's a good idea to use this until you get fully familiar with the operation of the store. It will prevent you accidentally ordering music that might destroy your musical credentials!

You'll notice when you come to choose a track to purchase that not all tracks are always available. With deference to those artists who have produced very long tracks, some may not be available for individual purchase; they'll be marked as 'Album Only'. To get these you'll have to purchase the whole album.

Completing an album

As we've said, a joy of iTunes is that you can browse the huge catalogue and find tracks from artists whose albums you probably wouldn't previously have considered buying. Sometimes after buying a track or two, do you wish you'd bought the whole album? That's a shame because you'd be reluctant to shell out for an album that contained the tracks you'd already purchased.

Thoughtfully, the Store has considered this and provides an option called 'Complete my Album'. Select this option (from the Quick Links) and you can purchase the remaining tracks of the album and pay a total price equivalent only to purchasing the album. In effect, the cost of the tracks you downloaded is credited back to you.

Purchasing movies, video and audiobooks

Want to add a movie, video or audiobook to your library? Well, the process is exactly the same. Access the respective Store department, make your choice and press the corresponding Purchase button. It's all automatic and seamless.

Subscribing to podcasts

The Store also plays host to a huge number of podcasts (tens, if not hundreds, of thousands) that range from professional productions from TV networks, often in support of TV broadcasts, through to amateur creations, produced by people armed with nothing more than a computer and microphone. In general, the most popular are condensed versions of radio shows, and here BBC broadcasts tend to lead the field.

The podcast window: like the main store window, that for the podcast department gives you a wide range of options as well as the chance to search for a specific entry.

Most podcasts are episodic and you can subscribe to them by hitting the Subscribe button. Now, every time a new episode is released, iTunes will find, download and make it available for you to enjoy.

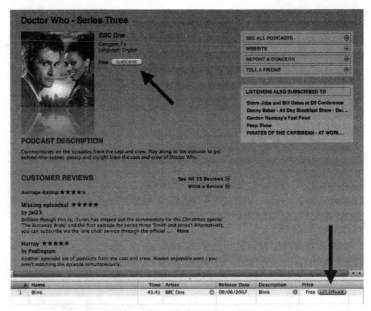

Click on the Get Episode button (bottom arrow) to download an individual podcast or Subscribe (upper arrow) to subscribe to a complete series.

Buying from iTunes Plus

You can buy, in the same way, from iTunes Plus, which offers DRM free audio at higher quality than standard tracks. If you already have a music collection, or have purchased some standard recordings, you can upgrade to the higher quality versions. Click on the Quick Link to iTunes Plus and iTunes will automatically show you which tracks can be upgraded and even work out the cost of upgrading all. You don't have to select all the tracks – you can just choose your favourites, and pay accordingly. The upgrade pricing is based on the difference between the price of an iTunes Plus track and that which you have already paid.

iTunes Plus will analyse which tracks in your collection can be upgraded, list them, and offer an upgrade price.

Using iTunes U

iTunes U – that's U for University – provides access to a wide range of course material on popular subjects in audio and video formats. You can think of these as enhanced podcasts. To view them, select the iTunes U department from the front page and browse the course material on offer. At the time of writing, most of this material is available free of charge, and lecture courses are, like some podcasts, available on a subscription basis.

iTunes U: a university course on your desktop, or iPod.

Synchronizing with your iPod

Now you've a flourishing music collection on your computer, you'll want to enjoy it everywhere via your iPod. So how do you transfer your music to it? Easy – it's an automatic process. Whenever you connect your iPod (and we're talking about the standard iPod) it will synchronize with your iTunes library, so that your iPod and library will be identical. Modify your library (by adding new tracks or deleting others) and the next time you connect, the modifications will be made to the iPod too.

The first time you connect your iPod you'll be greeted with the iPod Set up Assistant which will walk you through the process of linking your iPod to your iTunes music library. Make sure you select (if it's not already selected) the **Automatically sync songs and videos to my iPod** button. Check the second button, **Automatically sync photos to my iPod**, if you want to keep your photo collection synced too.

Manually adding music

You can manually add music if you wish. You might do this if your music collection is too large for the iPod or you simply want more control over what is transferred. In this case make sure the **Automatically sync songs and videos to my iPod** button is unchecked. Then you simply select songs or albums from your library and drag them to the iPod icon in the Sources window. Selected tracks will then be copied across.

Loading your iPod shuffle

The iPod shuffle was never meant to hold an entire music collection and (unless your collection is unusually small) you'll need to be selective about what is added. iTunes makes this easy by displaying a small window at the bottom of iTunes when you connect a shuffle. This lets you Autofill the shuffle – taking music randomly from your collection – or choose to automatically fill from a playlist. Playlists (which we will explore in detail in the next chapter) are collections of tracks that you can produce from your collection. You can also add tracks manually to a shuffle, either starting from scratch or to augment those tracks added using the Autofill feature. As before, simply drag tracks from your library to the iPod icon.

Preserving your investment

As your music library grows it will represent something of an investment both in time, putting it together, and money, with all those purchased tracks and other resources. That could all be lost should your computer fail. It makes good sense, then, to back up your collection periodically.

Depending on the size of your library you might want to create a backup copy on CDs, DVDs, Blu Ray discs or even a separate hard disc. In the latter case you can copy your whole iTunes library (a folder called iTunes) to the second disc. If you don't have a spare disc or you want to produce a second backup on CD or DVD then you can do so from the Preferences. Here's how:

1 In iTunes select **File > New Playlist** to create a new playlist.

2 Copy all your music tracks to this playlist.

3 Open the **iTunes preferences** and select **Advanced**.

4 Click on the **Data CD** button.

5 Click **OK**.

6 Select **File > Burn Playlist to Disc**.

To make a more thorough backup:

1 Select **File > Back Up to Disc**.

2 Select from the dialogue box (the options are **Entire Library**, **iTunes Store Purchases** or **Items added or changed since last backup**).

3 Feed in blank media when prompted. You can use any supported discs to complete the backup.

Summary

By now you should be able to start populating your iTunes music library with tracks and albums from your collection. You may even be importing old analogue recordings and giving them a new lease of life in the digital world. You should also be able – should you wish – to take out an account for the iTunes Store and enhance your own music collection with some new material – and not just music tracks. Though you can start enjoying this collection – both from your computer and your iPod – we have so far only set up the infrastructure. There's considerably more you can do with iTunes and your iPod. We'll explore some of these opportunities in the next chapter.

05

enjoying your digital music

In this chapter you will learn:

- how to navigate the iPod menus
- about playlists, iMixes and sharing music
- how to distribute your music around the home
- about taking music on the road

As you've probably guessed there's much more to iTunes and the iPod than we've touched on so far and now is the time to begin to explore some of the great features that'll help you enjoy it. In this chapter we'll take a look at playlists – the collections of music you can put together yourself – and how you can share these with friends and iTunes users around the globe. We'll also take a look at how you can free your music collection from the computer and its speakers and enjoy music all around the house. But why stop there? Wouldn't it be great if you could enjoy anything from your music collection anytime you're in your car too?

Navigating the iPod menus

Before we go any further it might be useful to get to grips with the iPod menus. Below we describe the principal ones and what the menu items do. Different models have slightly different arrangements (and the shuffle, perhaps obviously, doesn't have any) but the general layout and options are much the same.

One of the features that has made the iPod such a runaway success is the unique combination of controls and menus. There are few actual controls yet navigating the functions and menus remains amazingly simple. The thing to remember is that the iPod's top level menu is simply called 'iPod'. No matter how far down into the structure you go (and you use the centre button to delve deeper and make selections) you can return here by pressing – or pressing repeatedly – the Menu button on the click wheel. Let's look at the key menus.

The iPod menu

The **Music, Photos, Video, Extras** and **Settings** items access the menus of those names.

Shuffle Songs is a shortcut to shuffling your music collection.

Top: the classic iPod menu.

Below: in the iPod nano (video), the menus are combined on a split screen with random displays of artwork from your album and video collection.

The Music menu

All the audio options for your iPod (including audiobooks and podcasts as well as music) are accessed from within the Music menu.

Music
Playlists >
Artists >
Albums >
Songs >
Podcasts >
Genres >
Composers >
Audiobooks >
Search >

* **Playlists**: from here you can get a list of your playlists.

* **Artists**: lists all the songs in your collection alphabetically by the artist or performer's name.

* **Albums**: alphabetically lists your music by album name.

* **Songs**: alphabetically lists your music by song title.

* **Podcasts**: lists all the podcasts transferred to your iPod.

* **Genres**: your music collection arranged according to genre, such as rock, easy listening and so on.

* **Composers**: music arranged according to the songwriter.

* **Audiobooks**: listing of the audiobooks on your iPod.

* **Search**: lets you locate a specific track by using the initial few letters (selected from a small onscreen keyboard).

The Photos menu

If you have a photo library on your iPod, you can explore it from here.

* **Slideshow Settings**: opens the Slideshow settings menu – used to configure a slideshow for display on the iPod screen or a TV screen (see below).

* **Photo Library**: accesses the photo library directly.

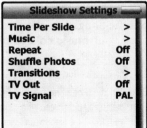

* **Individual albums**: any photo albums you've configured (think of these as the photo equivalent of playlists).

The Videos menu

If your iPod has video capabilities here's where you can view and control the content.

Videos

Video Playlists   >
Movies   >
Music Videos   >
TV Shows   >
Video Podcasts   >
Video Settings   >

73

enjoying your digital music 05

* **Video Playlists:** listed alphabetically.

* **Movies:** lists any movies you've downloaded to your iPod.

* **Music Videos:** in alphabetical order.

* **TV Shows:** any you have downloaded, listed alphabetically.

* **Video Podcasts:** any you have downloaded, listed alphabetically.

* **Video Settings:** playback options for TV replay, or to set a conventional-format iPod screen to playback in widescreen format.

The Settings menu

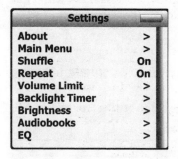

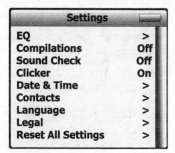

There are sufficient controls in the Settings menu to fill at least two screens. Here's what they all mean.

* **About:** all the information relevant to your iPod and the media stored on it.

* **Main Menu:** if you want to change or customize your iPod's main menu, you can do it from here.

* **Shuffle:** set to 'Off' or 'On', 'On' will shuffle your songs or albums in a random way.

- **Repeat:** set this to repeat either the current song indefinitely or all the current playlist.

- **Volume Limit:** locks the maximum output volume – to avoid the risk of ear damage.

- **Backlight Timer:** adjust the duration of the backlight – from one second to Always On.

- **Brightness:** change the screen brightness (most relevant to movies).

- **Audiobooks:** change the speed of the narrators' voice.

- **EQ:** change the equalizer presets to optimize playback for different music types.

- **Compilations:** when set to 'On' lets you add a Compilations submenu in the Music menu.

- **Sound Check:** helps to equalize sound levels between different tracks.

- **Clicker:** turn the clicking of the click wheel on or off.

- **Date & Time:** adjust the date and time shown on your iPod.

- **Contacts:** if you've synchronized an address book with your iPod you can switch the ordering of the names here.

- **Language:** displays menus in different languages (if you mess this up don't worry; Reset All Settings will remain in English).

- **Legal:** the iPod's equivalent to the tortuous licensing documents you agree to when loading software.

- **Reset All Settings:** returns all the menu settings to the original.

The Extras menu

Apart from music, movies, audiobooks et al., here you'll be able to access all the secondary resources on your iPod.

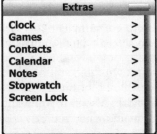

- **Clock:** turns your iPod into a clock display.

- **Games:** simple games are included on your iPod and others can be downloaded from the iTunes Store. Access them here.

- **Contacts:** you can copy your computer address book too and look up those contact details here.

- **Calendar:** the iPod calendar can sync with your calendar from iCal (Mac) or Outlook (Windows).

- **Notes:** use the inbuilt text reader to read notes and any copied documents.

- **Stopwatch:** more than just a clock, the iPod can also help time events and your daily workouts.

- **Screen Lock:** optional protection to stop others seeing your content.

Now Playing

This is whatever you are currently listening to. The display shows the album cover art, if available, the track, artist and album details along with the time into the track.

Playlists and music collections

With all your music loaded into your library it can turn into something of a monster. Hundreds, perhaps thousands of tracks, all vying for your attention. When you want to sit down and enjoy some music, what do you do? Start at the beginning? Or locate a specific album and start playing from there? Both methods are perfectly valid but it's unlikely (and, ultimately rather boring) to listen to your music in alphabetic, band, or even genre order.

That's why playlists are so important. When you create a playlist you can schedule and organize any music from your collection in any order. It's a bit like creating your own albums or creating your own radio station, though without the DJs or the interruptions you'd normally expect. Why might you create a playlist? For any reason. You might create one to burn a CD for playback in the car, or to set the mood for a party.

The great thing about playlists is that once you've created one, it's not only on iTunes on your computer. The next time you synchronize with your iPod, it'll be transferred there too. Note that when you create a playlist you're not copying the music files themselves to the list – they remain in the main library – so you can create as many playlists (and playlists as long as you like) without fear of filling up your iPod's memory. Think of the track titles in the playlist as being merely shortcuts or pointers to the original track.

Creating a playlist

You can create a new playlist by selecting **File > New Playlist**. A new, empty playlist will appear in the playlist section of the Sources window with the name 'untitled playlist'. You should now give your playlist a memorable name such as 'Party Mix', 'Easy Listening' or whatever will help you locate it later, on your computer or iPod.

To fill your playlist, select songs from your library and drag them on to that playlist icon on the Sources menu. You could select individual tracks, a set of tracks, or all the tracks in your collection (you'd do this to help create backups on disc; you can burn playlists to disc but not the library per se). To select multiple tracks, [Control]-click on each one you want to add.

You can also create a playlist by making selections of multiple tracks (using control-click again to add tracks to your selection) and then choose **File > New Playlist from Selection**. All your selections are added to a new playlist. You can now name the playlist accordingly. Mac users can use a shortcut here: select the tracks you want for the playlist, and drag them to the sources window, in the area of the existing playlists. If you don't drop them into an existing playlist iTunes presumes you want to create a new playlist and will do so for you.

Modifying a playlist

Once you've created a playlist you can modify it. You can:

+ add additional tracks
+ delete selected tracks
+ rearrange the order of tracks.

To add tracks simply drag them from the library to the playlist icon, as you did when creating a playlist. To delete a track select it by clicking on it and pressing [Delete] or [Backspace]. You can select multiple tracks to delete at the same time if you wish.

To rearrange the order of tracks in a playlist (tracks are normally listed in the order that you added them to the list) you can select one and drag it to the position you want. Release the mouse button and it will be inserted at the chosen location.

Smart playlists

Here's a neat little feature that you'll only appreciate after you've experienced it in action: Smart Playlists. When you create one (**File > New Smart Playlist**) you don't fill it with tracks. Instead you tell iTunes what type of music you want to add. To make this easier, iTunes displays a dialogue box that lets you specify criteria for the music you want included.

There are a wide range of criteria: you can specify, for example, on the basis of an artist name, album name, the date added to your collection, kind, genre and so on. You can even specify multiple criteria: such as music of a certain genre downloaded after a specific date and at a high bit rate. Then all the tracks corresponding to those rules will be listed in the playlist. Any new tracks you download that correspond to the rules will also be added.

As you explore the options, you'll see how much fun this can be. For example, you could select to group together in a playlist all those tracks from your favourite artist that you haven't listened to in the last year. Or all the tracks you've downloaded but haven't got round to listening to yet.

Preconfigured playlists

You may have noticed when you create new playlists that there are actually some already listed. These are essentially Smart Playlists and include (and bear in mind this list does change):

+ **Music Videos** – a repository for your music videos.

+ **My Top Rated** – iTunes lets you rate music. Your top rated tracks are added here.

+ **Recently Added** – those tracks you've recently added.

- **Recently Played** – tracks you've been listening to recently.
- **Top 25 Most Played** – the 25 tracks you've played most often.

The Party Shuffle playlist

For that long party session, you can let iTunes create a super-playlist called the Party Shuffle. This will normally take music at random from your library or you can use the Source drop-down menu to select music from a specific playlist (usually the better option if your library contains a wide and diverse range of music). It can also bias the choices towards those tracks that you rate more highly.

What you can do with playlists

We've mentioned that you can use a playlist to burn a CD or to help back up your iTunes library. What else can you do? Well, you can:

- Listen to your playlists on the computer that stores your iTunes library.
- Let the users of other computers in your home share the playlists and listen to them on their own computers (more about this later).
- Sync your playlists with your iPod, iTunes compatible phone or iPhone.
- Share your playlist as an iMix on the iTunes Store for others to share.

Transferring a playlist to an iPod

All the playlists you create will be automatically transferred to your iPod the next time you synchronize it with iTunes. That's assuming, like most users, you'll have the synchronization process set to autosync (the default setting).

If you have any problems, follow these instructions:

1 Connect your iPod to your computer.
2 Select the **iPod** icon in iTunes when it appears (iTunes will open automatically if it is not already open).

3 Click on the **Summary** tab.

4 Ensure that the **Manually Manage Music** or **Manually manage music and video** button is not selected.

5 Click on the **Music** tab and select **Sync Music** and **All songs and playlists**. This will ensure all songs, and all playlists, are transferred on every synchronization. You can select **Selected Playlists** if you want only selected playlists to be synchronized.

On the iPod shuffle, due to its limited capacity, you'll generally use Autofill from a selected playlist.

The On-The-Go playlist

There's one kind of playlist you don't create in iTunes: it's called the On-The-Go playlist. Imagine you're on a long journey with your iPod, enjoying your music collection. You've got some interesting playlists but then decide that you'd prefer a different selection. The On-The-Go playlist feature lets you assemble a playlist on the spot – and on your iPod – and save that for syncing back to iTunes next time you synchronize.

You can build an On-The-Go playlist simply.

1 Scroll through your music collection and when you reach a tune you want to select, hold down the iPod's centre button until the title starts flashing. That song is added.

2 Repeat the process with as many songs as you want to add to the playlist.

3 Then press the iPod's menu button until you are at the **Music** menu and select **Playlists > On-The-Go**. You'll see all the songs you've added.

4 Check that they are all as you remembered them, then select **Save Playlist** to save, or **Clear Playlist** to (obviously) clear it.

In the absence of a screen you can't create On-The-Go playlists with an iPod shuffle.

iMixes: publishing your playlist

When you've created a playlist you may think it – and your skill and judgement in selecting tracks – needs further exposure. In this case why not publish your playlist in the iTunes Store? With iTunes you can publish your playlist as an iMix – and add some notes to explain your choices. Once you've created your iMix anyone visiting the store can get to see it. You're not making the songs available to all and sundry: anyone that views your selections as an iMix and likes it can audition the tracks you've listed but, if they want to enjoy them in full, they have to purchase them. So it's good business for the iTunes Store and good publicity for you. How do you create one? Simple. Here's how.

1 Sign in to your iTunes Store account.

2 Select the playlist you want to publish as an iMix from those in the source window.

3 Select **File > Create an iMix** and work your way through the on-screen instructions.

4 When complete with your comments and notes, click the **Publish** button.

Note that if any of the music in your iMix is not available through the Store (perhaps something you ripped from a hard-to-find CD) they won't appear in the iMix. That has caused consternation for some whose elegant, well-conceived playlist containing rare, hard-to-find music becomes shorter and more mainstream when published.

Essentials, collections and originals

The guys at iTunes have been pretty busy compiling what amounts to their own iMixes – thematic collections of music that they promote as extended albums. They cover all genres and all interests: for example, you'll find titles such as 90s Pop, The Sounds of London and Holiday Specials. You'll find a shortcut to these – *iTunes Collections* – from the front page of the iTunes Store.

Essentials is another iTunes collection – this time more specific. They take the form of a three-level approach to the music in question starting with the more popular works, then going for some of the less well-known and rounding off with some of the better but more obscure output. Again you can access iTunes Essentials from the shortcut on the Store homepage. Look out for artist-based essentials, historical (such as World Music, 80s 12inch mixes and Trance) and even more personal collections (Fitness, Father's Day and Party, a few amongst many).

Finally, amongst these collections come *iTunes Originals*: works by contemporary artists that generally include an exclusive live session. Interspersed with the tracks – and sometimes video too – are commentaries and insights into the artists themselves.

Your music around the house

With such a great resource as your iTunes library you'll want to enjoy it everywhere. That's where the iPod comes in. But, and for some it's a big but, you don't necessarily want to be glued to your headphones when around the house. Of course, there's an alternative: you can connect your iPod directly to a home hifi and enjoy your music via its speakers.

Discovering AirTunes

There's a more elegant solution, though, one that Apple call AirTunes. AirTunes is a way of configuring a remote (remote from your computer, that is) set of speakers to replay your music and using your home wireless network to distribute it. Apple released a pocket-sized wireless hub called Airport Express for this very purpose, although you can create an AirTunes network using any standard wireless hubs.

It doesn't matter where your speakers are located – in your lounge, kitchen or bedroom – or where your computer is installed. All you need to do to configure a network is connect your hifi (or your hifi speakers, if they are self-powered) into the Airport Express using a standard audio cable. Once the connection is made, iTunes will detect the connection and you'll see a new pop-up box in the iTunes window. The new speaker connection will be listed and, when you select it, anything you select on iTunes will play out through those speakers.

Note that if you have a wireless hub already installed elsewhere in the house you don't need to replace this or move it to the vicinity of the speakers. You can add an Airport Express at a location convenient to the hifi and that – and the old hub – will communicate.

The Squeezebox and Soundbridge

The drawback with the original AirTunes solutions, elegant though it might have been, was that it played only the music selected in iTunes – that is, whatever playlist was selected at the time. What if you wanted to have more control over your networked music? Or you wanted to see what was playing?

That's the rationale for the Squeezebox and the Soundbridge. Both these devices can connect with iTunes remotely and to speakers via a wired connection. Then you can see what you are listening to and have control over what is playing. One limitation both share is the inability to replay DRM protected music such as the standard fare you'll purchase from iTunes. Purchases from iTunes Plus (which don't feature DRM) will play out just fine.

Squeezebox (above) and Soundbridge (right): compact, but with a clear display, these devices are a great way to enjoy (and control) your iTunes library around the home.

In the car

It's surprising – or perhaps it isn't – how our expectations of music on the move have changed. When crackly AM radio gave way to FM an increasing number of speakers around the acoustically hostile environment of a car interior delivered very much improved sound. Dissatisfied with radio we would produce tape compilations and latterly, enjoy CDs. But, despite CD jukeboxes that can play any one of up to 10 CDs we still can't get enough. After some time with your iPod your expectations will be set even higher. So, what about taking your iPod with you, and replay the music through the car hifi? No problem – in fact, there are a number of solutions to using your iPod in the car.

The direct connection

The easiest is that found in a number of more recent vehicles. You can connect your iPod directly, as wily manufacturers have incorporated an iPod connection into the car's electronics. Connect your iPod and you are all set to play your music. The level of connectivity does vary – in some cases you can play the music through the audio system, but not control it. In other (admittedly the premium brands) you can also control your iPod via the car audio's controls.

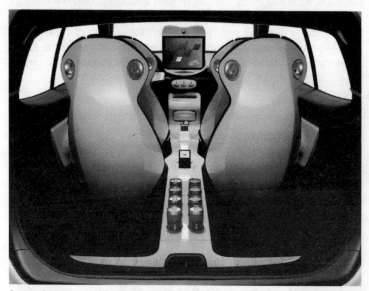

Centre of attention: this Renault concept car puts the iPod in the centre of the dashboard. A case of plug and go.

The tape adaptor

If your car doesn't have the direct connection you can still exploit your car audio by using a cassette adaptor. These have been around for years and were previously used to allow personal CD players to play through the audio system. It comprises a compact cassette shell that you insert into your car's tape slot. Leading from this is a cable that you connect to your iPod. The adaptor cassette feeds a signal from the iPod through the tape heads and into the audio system, kidding the system into thinking it's replaying a tape.

Before investing in one take a close look at your car's audio unit. Some have a minijack socket on the front, or the option of connecting one to the back of the unit. In these cases you can cut out the cassette adaptor altogether and link your iPod to the audio system using a cheap minijack-to-minijack cable.

The FM solution

Not all audio systems today feature tape decks (and one has to ask now, how long will the CD remain a feature?), so what then? You can go for an FM-based solution. By connecting an FM transmitter – a small unit you can attach to the dock or your iPod – you can transmit the music over the air just like a miniature radio station. You then tune your car's radio to the corresponding frequency and there your are: your music!

FM solutions – such as the iTrip or RoadTrip from Griffin Technology – offer an easy-to-use, wireless solution. The drawbacks? They can be prone to interference (particularly if there is a radio station broadcasting on a similar frequency). You may have to retune your system periodically as you travel the country.

A second problem, common to the tape adaptor and some of the other solutions, is that you may also need to provide a way of charging the iPod on the road. Some FM solutions come with cradles that link to the dashboard power outlet but for those that don't you'll have to equip yourself with an extra cable.

FM Transmitters: this FM transmitter lets you transmit your iPod's music to your car radio. The charging lead ensures the iPod's batteries are topped up at all times.

After market kits

The tape and FM solutions are great if you regularly use two or more vehicles. Even if you rent a car you can take your iPod sound system with you. However, if you want something more permanent and more effective, you can have a professional installation that will mirror those found in factory installed solutions. These can be expensive – there's a fair amount of electronics to account for – but if you want the best in sound quality, this is the way to go.

This car kit from Harmon/Kardon can be fitted to just about any car and allows full control – along with visual feedback – of your iPod.

Summary

The essence of the iPod is that it's a simple-to-use device but capable of almost limitless expansion. Throw iTunes into the mix and you've an incredible resource. You'll have seen now how the menu system on your iPod manages to be simple, yet comprehensive. There is a great deal within the menus but for normal operation you can get to your favourite music in just a couple of clicks. You will also have seen how you can enjoy your music more through the creation of playlists. Far from being an extra source of music your iPod and iTunes can now supplant your existing music systems around the home and when you are out on your road.

So is that it? Most definitely not! The scope and reach of the iPod and iTunes is growing all the time and that growth means more goodies for us all. In the next chapter we'll take a look as some more – some obvious, some less so – things that you can do armed with an iPod.

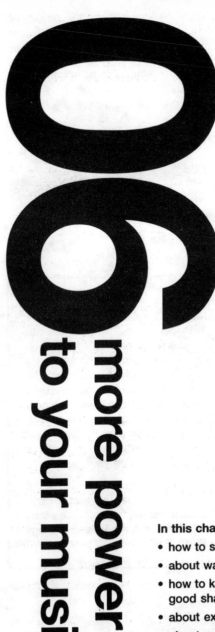

06 more power to your music

In this chapter you will learn:

- how to share your music
- about ways of gifting music
- how to keep your library and iPod in good shape
- about exporting music
- about creating CDs and CD artwork
- about iTunes radio

We have concentrated – so far – on some of the mechanics of iTunes and the iPod. You'll have discovered how much fun it can be creating libraries of music and listening to them on your iPod or hifi. But there's even more to both your iPod and iTunes that we've yet to discover and we'll explore these through this chapter.

Caring and sharing

Let's begin by taking a look at how we can share our music with others and how they can reciprocate by sharing their music with you.

Sharing your iTunes library

If you were proud of your conventional music collection, chances are you'll be especially proud of your new digital version. As well as having all your original material (or perhaps your pick of the best) you'll probably have added some new tracks courtesy of the iTunes Store. So why not share it? We saw in the last chapter how you can stream your music wirelessly to a hifi for example, but you can also share your collection with other family members with computers that share the same network. Here's how.

To make your iTunes library visible – and accessible – to others on your network you need to open the iTunes Preferences (a useful shortcut for this is [Control]-[comma] on a Windows PC or [Apple key]-[comma] on a Mac). Click on the **Sharing** tab at the top of the screen and click the appropriate boxes. Click:

- **Look for shared libraries:** to detect and display any other people's iTunes libraries.
- **Share my library on my local network:** to share your iTunes library with any other computers on your computer network.
- **Share entire library:** to share everything in your library.
- **Share selected playlists:** to share only the playlists that you select in the pane below.

If you wish, you can give your shared library a name (such as 'Dad's Library', 'Sarah's Library') and specify a password. You might want to restrict content if, for example, there are tracks with explicit lyrics. Note that the Shared Name option appears in the General Preferences in some versions of iTunes.

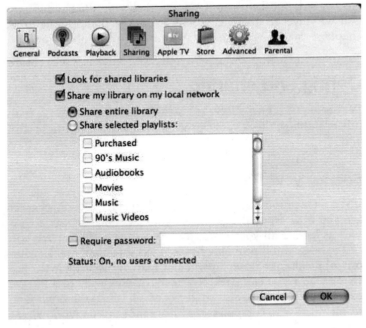

Sharing libraries: you can configure your sharing of libraries amongst computers on the network in the Preferences.

Once you've set up sharing, any or all of the people on the network can access each others' iTunes libraries by selecting the respective library name from the sources window. So, is it the same as having multiple copies of the one library? No. If you access a shared library you can't add any of the items to your own library (or playlists) nor can you copy it to a CD or even an iPod. Think of it more as guest access.

Authorizing and deauthorizing your computer

You probably won't have discovered until you try sharing, that you can only play your music collection on an authorized computer. By default, the computer you have used to create your original iTunes library will be authorized to play back any music (or other media) you purchased from the iTunes Store. For your music to play on another computer you will need to authorize that one too. This may be another computer you have around the home or your work computer. Authorize that and you'll be able to enjoy your music collection at the office too. You can have up to five computers authorized at any one time and these can be Macintoshes, Windows or a combination.

To authorize a computer to play your Store purchases select **Store > Authorize Computer...** You'll need to provide your account details to complete the activation. What happens if you try to authorize a sixth computer? You'll be blocked; if you wish to activate that computer you'll have to deauthorize (**Store > Deauthorize Computer...**) one first.

It's important that if you sell or trash an old computer that you deauthorize it first. Otherwise, even though it is no longer yours, or no longer exists, it will still count towards your five authorized computers. If you did forget to deauthorize, there is a catch-all solution. You can view your account details (choose **Store > View My Account**) and deauthorize all your computers. You can then authorize (or reauthorize) all those that you want to use. Note that you can only use this emergency fix once per calendar year.

Once you've set up the authorizations you can copy the files to the newly authorized computer by copying them to CD or DVD, using an intermediate hard disc or even copying the respective files over the network. Note that authorization is only necessary for store purchases: other files can be copied between your computers without the need to authorize.

Once they are on the second computer, the files can be dragged from the CD or DVD and dropped into the library window of iTunes. They will then be imported and ready to be enjoyed. You can also copy the files first, without authorizing: then the first time you try to play them you'll be prompted for your Apple ID and password.

A short cut for copying between authorized computers

Normally you can't download a library from an iPod to a computer. But what if you have two authorized computers and you've downloaded tracks on each? If you were to synchronize your iPod with each computer you'd only have the tracks from one on the iPod at any one time. Is there any way that you can consolidate your purchases into a single library? Yes. Here's how.

1 Begin by connecting your iPod to your first computer and synchronize it with the iTunes library on that computer.

2 Disconnect the iPod from that computer and attach it to the second computer.

3 Before synchronizing with the second computer select **File > Transfer Purchases** from '*iPod name*'.

Purchased items loaded on to the iPod from the first iTunes library will now be added to the library of the second computer. Note that this transfer method only applies to items purchased from the iTunes Store, not any other material you may have in the original library.

Parental controls

You can imagine that, with time, your iTunes library can grow as a great family resource. There will be all your family's favourite music, some audio books, TV programmes, videos and more. But with that comes problems. What if you don't want your children (or your maiden aunt who is staying for the weekend) downloading huge back catalogues or explicit material? Fortunately that's been thought of in the Parental Controls pane of the Preferences.

You'll see that this gives you the option to:

• Disable access to podcasts and Internet radio. Select this and the respective icons won't be shown in the source list window.

• Fully disable access to the iTunes Store. It too will no longer be shown in the source list window.

• Disable any shared libraries.

• Restrict movies visible in the store to a specific age certificate.

• Do the same for television programmes where such certification exists.

• Restrict explicit content. This applies to all explicit material listed in the store and includes all those lyrics that are so identified by their respective publishers.

Parental Control

| General | Podcasts | Playback | Sharing | Apple TV | Store | Advanced | Parental |

Sources: ☐ Disable Podcasts
☐ Disable Radio
☑ Disable iTunes Store
☑ Disable Shared Libraries

Ratings for: United Kingdom ⬦

iTunes Store: ☑ Restrict movies to PG ⬦
☐ Restrict TV shows to N/A ⬦
☑ Restrict explicit content

🔓 Click the lock to prevent further changes.

Cancel   OK

Parental controls let you keep prying eyes – and ears – away from contentious materials.

Gift cards, certificates and allowances

If you know family members or friends have their own iTunes libraries, you can take advantage of some simple ways that Apple have provided for you to gift music to them.

Gift certificates allow you to gift an amount of money for the recipient to spend as they wish in the iTunes Store. When you

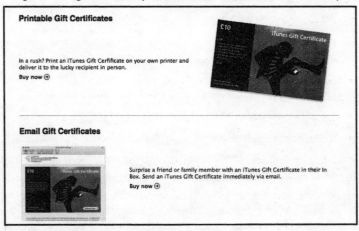

Printable Gift Certificates

In a rush? Print an iTunes Gift Certificate on your own printer and deliver it to the lucky recipient in person.
Buy now ⊕

Email Gift Certificates

Surprise a friend or family member with an iTunes Gift Certificate in their In Box. Send an iTunes Gift Certificate immediately via email.
Buy now ⊕

iTunes gift certificates: an ideal gift for the iTunes lover.

buy a certificate you can choose to have it delivered by e-mail or, if you want to make it a bit more personal, in person by printing out the certificate.

You can purchase one from the front page of the iTunes Store. Click on **Buy iTunes Gifts** in the Quick Links section and choose from a printable certificate or an e-mail delivered one. You'll be asked to complete a couple of pages of information along with a personalized message. When everything is done, you can have the certificate sent, or print it out.

To redeem a certificate, all you need do is click on the **Redeem** option (in the Quick Links panel) and follow the instructions. It involves nothing more than copying the certificate number in to the respective box. Then you can go on a wild shopping spree, or wait and make some considered purchases later.

Gift cards work in a similar way except you can purchase a card from a number of online retailers and quite a few bricks-and-mortar stores too. The card – in the form of a physical, credit card – features a number that you can redeem in exactly the same way as you would a gift certificate.

Allowance accounts are a more targeted way to allow family members, particularly, to make purchases. This time rather than a fixed gifted amount, you can set a monthly allowance that the

🔒 Secure Connection

Set up an iTunes Monthly Gift

An iTunes monthly gift provides a simple way for family members and friends to buy music without giving them your payment card. Monthly gifts can be purchased in amounts from £5.00 to £100.00. Recipients must have an Apple account for use in the UK store, which you can easily set up below. Monthly gifts may be cancelled at any time by visiting your Account Info page.

Your Name:	Peter
Recipient's Name:	
Monthly Gift:	£10.00 ⬦ from £5.00 to £100.00
First Installment:	○ Don't send now, wait until the first of next month ● Send now, and on the first of next month
Recipient's Apple ID:	○ Create an Apple Account for recipient ● Use recipient's existing Apple Account
Apple ID:	
Verify Apple ID:	
Personal Message:	

(Cancel)　(Continue)

Set up allowance accounts from the Buy iTunes gifts option in the quick links window.

lucky recipient can spend in the Store. When they reach their limit their spending comes to a stop until the account is replenished the next month. An allowance account requires that the payee and the payer both have an Apple or iTunes account.

A final option for the philanthropist is the iTunes Gift feature, which lets you gift a specific track, video or movie – or indeed anything from the store. To start the process click the **Gift this Music** button that you'll see adjacent to the conventional purchase button.

Wishlists

If you've gifted away so much money for others to enjoy in the iTunes store that you're left a little short yourself, you could consider making a wishlist. This lets you compile a list of all those tracks (and other media) you are considering buying. When you add a track to a wishlist you also add its 30-second preview (the same one that you normally listen to when auditioning tracks) as an aide memoire.

Building a wishlist is advisable for those who start browsing the store late at night. Many of us have woken the next morning to find that we've purchased the entire collection from the last twenty years of Eurovision (or something equally damning); putting them in a wishlist first lets you consider your choices the next day and filter out all those that common sense dictates shouldn't be on the list.

How do you create one? Make a new playlist and give it a name like 'Wishlist' (though you can have as many as you like running concurrently). Then, as you audition music, drag the tracks from the Store to the icon. The audition preview – along with all the attached information – will be saved to your wishlist.

Good housekeeping

On the whole you'll find iTunes is a very well behaved application. It will sit there delivering your music day after day and, when you want to be a bit more proactive, let you search and download from its amazing catalogue. Now and again it may not work exactly as expected. In those (actually very rare) situations, help is close at hand.

Interrupted downloads

Get familiar with the Music Store, and downloading purchases – or free resources – can get addictive. Best of all, it happens with just a few clicks of the mouse. Without any intervention on your part, chosen selections appear in your iTunes library. But what if something goes wrong during the download process, say your Internet connection goes down, or you have a power failure? iTunes will download your purchases only once (which is why it is vital to keep a backup especially of purchased items) so have you lost your new purchases? Thankfully not. Once you've re-established a connection with iTunes the downloading should continue from where it left off.

If it doesn't, there's a fall-back position. Select **Store > Check For Purchases.** Your computer will check with the Store what purchases have been fully downloaded and which have not. If the tally between your computer and the Store is different (indicating that a purchase – or purchases – have not been received in full) the Store will be prompted to continue with, or re-initiate, the downloading.

Keeping an eye on your iTunes purchases

The iTunes Store can be so compelling that it is easy to lose track of what you've purchased. Fortunately iTunes provides two ways for you to keep tabs on them. First, in the Sources window, just below the iTunes Store icon is a Purchased icon. Click on this and you can take a look at a listing of all the purchases made.

If you want something more detailed you can produce a report on those purchases. This is a good way to keep a check on your whole iTunes account – so it's ideal for checking on whether anyone else in the family has been sneaking some downloads on your account.

You can find this information by visiting the iTunes Store homepage and clicking on Account in the Quick Links. When you see your account information, click on Purchase History.

You'll see a full listing of your purchases, in reverse chronological order. If you are checking up because you suspect misuse of your account (and by that we mean by someone other than family members or those authorized by you to access your account) you can hit the Report a Problem button to highlight and report any suspicious activity.

Remember too that you will get an email receipt of any purchases you make – these don't arrive straight after purchase but may be a day or two later and include all the purchases made in a period. Each emailed invoice corresponds to a line entry in the purchase history report.

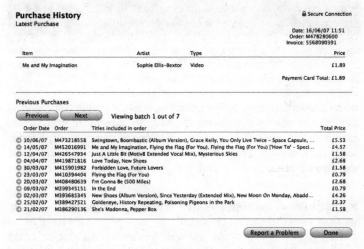

Purchase history: want an overview of your iTunes Store spending? Suspect junior has been downloading the latest Green Day albums? The Purchase History page will detail all purchases on your account.

Album Artwork

When you download an album or a track from the iTunes Store you also get a copy of the artwork – generally comprising the album cover – downloaded and displayed at the bottom of the Sources window. Subsequently, you can choose to display either the artwork of the track currently playing or any item you have selected from the library listing. The same cover art also appears in the CoverFlow if you've set your library (or playlists) to display in this format.

If you've filled your library with tracks ripped from your CDs you won't have this artwork as a matter of course. That doesn't mean that you will need to go without. If you have an iTunes

CoverFlow: when you download music you also get the album artwork, displayed in Coverflow. Tracks that don't currently feature cover art display are shown as a blank square with a music note (left of centre artwork here).

Store account (even if you've never made any purchases) you can send it off on a mission to find the cover art that corresponds to the music that, in artwork terms, is currently orphaned. Select **Advanced > Get Album Artwork** and iTunes will head off onto the Internet and try and seek out the artwork corresponding to your albums.

You will get a warning prior to the search beginning – this is because to get the artwork, details of your purchases have to be sent to Apple. There's nothing sinister here – it's just to cross reference with databases of images and this information is neither stored nor used for any other purpose. But, if you are unhappy with this you might want to choose a different, manual method of adding artwork (below).

How long does the search take? That depends on the size of the library. Expect it to take a few minutes but if it takes longer don't worry. It may need to do a little more detective work.

If the automatic process of finding album artwork fails (and that's quite possible – there will be many albums and tracks that don't yet feature in album art galleries) you can add the artwork yourself.

To do this:

1 Select an image that corresponds to the track. Most people make their way to Amazon or another site offering images of album covers and grab an image from there.

2 When you find the album cover remember to click on the **Show Larger Image** link to get the best quality image.

3 Drag this image to your computer desktop.

4 Select the corresponding track in iTunes. Make sure that the **Selected Item** box is open at the bottom of the source window (it will show the message 'Drag Album Artwork Here') .

5 Drag the image icon from your desktop to this window and drop it in.

6 In a few seconds the cover art will appear here and, if selected, in the CoverFlow view of your library.

Incidentally, the image you add doesn't have to be the album cover – you can add any image. Should you wish – and I'm a bit pressed to see a reason why – you can add several images to a track and click your way through them.

Exporting from iTunes and your iPod

So far all our efforts and attentions have gone into getting music (and more) into iTunes and into iPods. But you can also get your music out. You might want to produce your own audio mix CD, for example, or (should the worst happen) need to recover your iTunes library from your iPod.

Creating music CDs

iTunes lets you create two kinds of music CD: audio and MP3. Audio CDs are the conventional CDs akin to those that you might purchase at a music store. MP3 CDs feature music recorded as compact MP3 files rather than the more space hungry AIFF format used with conventional CDs. That means you can cram on up to ten times as much music as you can on a standard CD. The drawback is that not all CD players can play these discs; car CD players are the most likely to accept them.

As we've mentioned earlier when discussing backing up to CDs, you can't copy your library – or library items – directly to CD. Instead you need to create a playlist containing those tracks you want to burn to CD. It's a good idea, when doing this, to make a quick check on the number of tracks in the list, and the duration. As a rule of thumb, a standard CD will accommodate up to 15 standard tracks, or up to 75 minutes of music. The MP3 disc will hold around 12 hours of music or 150 tracks.

To create a CD you will first need to visit the Preferences window and select whether you want the disc to be an MP3 CD or a conventional one. In the case of the latter you can also specify a gap to be added between songs and whether to use sound checking. Sound checking is a useful feature if you've gathered together a selection of tracks from different original albums. It will ensure that the volume of the compiled CD is constant and you don't get tracks that are particularly loud or quiet.

Now you are all set to burn your disc:

1   Begin by selecting the playlist you want to burn to CD. Check, as we noted above, that you're within the nominal capacity of the disc and that your compiled tracks are in the order that you'd like to hear them on the finished disc. If not you can drag and drop them into the correct order.

2   Select **File > Burn Playlist to Disc,** or click the **Burn Disc** button at the base of the iTunes window.

3   Add a blank CD (if you haven't already inserted one) and wait for the burn.

You can burn your CD by making a menu selection or clicking the Burn Disc button.

It may take a little longer than you are used to when burning a CD. Whether you choose a conventional CD or an MP3 disc, iTunes will need to convert the files from the iTunes AAC format to AIFF (for a standard CD) or MP3 (for the MP3 disc). You will get visual feedback, so keep an eye on the LCD panel at the top of the iTunes window to monitor progress.

CD artwork

Once you've created your CD you might want to create an insert for the CD case. ITunes has second-guessed you and provides all the tools you need to make professional looking artwork for your new compilation.

To print your CD cover artwork select **Print** from the **File** menu. You'll see a dialogue box as shown below. The drop-down menu in the dialogue box provides a range of different styles for your CD case insert. You can choose a simple, text-only insert or a colour mosaic that comprises thumbnail images produced from the artwork from the individual tracks. Make your choice and print. Your printout will feature cutting marks so that you can quickly trim to make a perfect sized insert.

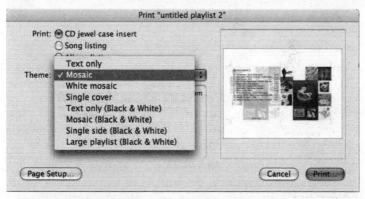

CD case insert: print a professional-looking insert for your CD compilation using iTunes Print utility.

The same print dialogue box will also let you print a song listing from the chosen playlist or an album listing.

Printing a CD

Sadly, iTunes doesn't (or doesn't as yet) allow you to create a graphic to print on the top surface of your CD. However, if you have burned your compilation on to a printable CD you can use the printing utilities that came with your inkjet printer (assuming it permits CD printing) to create a CD label or print directly on the CD.

Extracting music from your iPod

Consider this: you've been syncing your iPod and iTunes regularly but you've forgotten to backup your computer. Something catastrophic happens and you lose all the data on your computer. After a great deal of heartache, hair tearing and hassle you manage to reinstall all the essential software. Turning to your iTunes music collection for some light relief you discover to your horror that it's empty.

No matter, all your music is saved on your iPod. Sync your iPod and iTunes and all will be restored, right? No, and don't do it! Though some information is sent from the iPod to iTunes (On-The-Go playlists, for example) syncing will copy your new iTunes library to the iPod. Result? Nothing. Your empty library will now be on your iPod too.

With the exception of iTunes Store purchased music on commonly authorized computers, Apple prevents you copying your iPod collection from iPods to iTunes. That makes some sense; otherwise everyone would be sharing their iPod and iTunes collections and probably inadvertently circumventing every piece of music copyright legislation. And the limitation was probably dictated by those publishers that provide content to iTunes.

Of course, we can all understand the rationale for this but it can, under the exceptional circumstances we've already noted, prevent legitimate music owners from retrieving their purchases from their iPod. Fortunately, not encumbered by limitations in the same way as Apple, third parties have been quick to produce utilities that will allow you to recover your music should the worst happen.

You can find out what is currently available by using your web browser to search (try 'copy music from iPod to iTunes' in the search field) but here are some utilities you might want to consider:

For Windows versions of iTunes:

- PodUtil: (shareware) offers a free trial before you purchase.

- PodRip: (shareware) helps recover all the songs and playlists; also offers a free trial and is also available for Macintosh computers.

- PodPlus: (shareware) was originally a freeware product but now has additional functionality.

For Macintosh versions of iTunes:

- PodRip: (shareware) as described above.

- Senuti: a free utility that makes repairs easy thanks to its iTunes-like interface.

- iPod.iTunes: (shareware) handles music and video.

Making a good thing better: updates and upgrades

Apple is continually making iTunes better. Sometimes we see this when a new version is announced. Sometimes the improvements are more discrete and may be designed to overcome some operational anomalies (for that read bug-fixes).

To check for any current updates:

1 Select **Help > Check for Updates**. You'll then be given the option of installing any update detected.

To set iTunes to detect updates automatically:

1 For this select **Edit > Preferences > General**.

2 Click on **Check for updates automatically**.

If you are using a Macintosh, you'll be alerted to any software updates automatically as part of the Software Update system. If this is set up, you'll be advised of any updates to iTunes if available (along with any other software updates) every week or so. You can manually check by selecting **Apple > Check for updates**.

Updates appear too for your iPod. This may be to fix any bugs but often it's to add additional functionality. To ensure your iPod is up to date you need to do the following:

1 Connect your iPod to the computer you normally synchronize with.

2 Select **Help > Check for Updates** (Windows) or **Apple > Check for Updates** (Mac).

3 If your iPod is currently up to date you'll be advised in a dialogue box. If not you'll be prompted to download the new software.

4 Follow the onscreen instructions to install the software. In particular you'll be told at the end that the iPod is restarting (much as a computer sometimes needs to restart after installing new software).

5 Keep the iPod connected until told it is safe to disconnect.

Radio on iTunes

As well as being the repository for all your chosen music, iTunes is also a gateway to the world of Internet radio. You'll find the radio stations by clicking on the Radio button in the Sources window. This will show you all the genres of radio stations available. Click on any of these to see the radio stations on offer.

Often you'll see two versions of each, differentiated only by their bit rate. Choose the low bit rate version if you have a slow Internet connection and the higher one if you have broadband. Obviously with a higher bit rate you'll get better quality sound; but if you do have a slow connection you are likely to get better replay with less interruptions as your Internet connection struggles to keep pace with the incoming signal.

Is this the same as DAB Radio? No, this is Internet streamed radio. Some of the stations may be the same as you might receive on a DAB radio network but the delivery technology is quite different. Quality, however, particularly at the higher bit rate is often very similar.

Summary

After reading this chapter you should be more confident in using iTunes. We've taken a look at some of the house-keeping features that will keep your library and resources in tip-top condition, though, to be fair, iTunes does do a good job of looking after itself. You'll also know a great deal more about the social aspects of iTunes: how you can share your music collection and enjoy that of others in your family. You'll even know how to allow – or control – your family's spending in the iTunes Store! We've also taken the opportunity to look at what to do if – and it is if – things go wrong. In particular, how to download media from your iPod. This is very much a last resort, and shouldn't be regarded as an alternative to proper backing up procedures.

So far we've been rather focused on iTunes – and the iPod – as a music service. Next we'll take a look at how both handle visual media – photos and video.

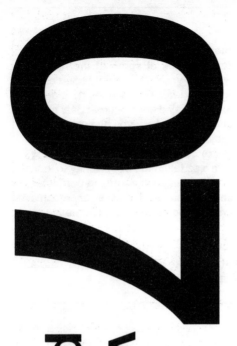

07

video and photos

In this chapter you will learn:

- how to store photos and video
- how to import video into iTunes
- about creating slideshows on your iPod and TV
- how you can enjoy missed TV shows
- about enjoying your videos on a TV
- about Apple TV

It's a testament to the original concept of the iPod that with just a modest upgrade, new models were able to handle pictures and video in exactly the same way as music – simply and effectively. In this chapter we'll take a look at what the iPod has to offer in the video, and photo, departments. Even if you'd never intended to use your iPod for anything other than music, you may find yourself strongly persuaded otherwise.

Taking your photo collection with you

You may recall from Chapter 1 that towards the end of 2004 the iPod first gained a colour screen and the ability to store and display photos. Since then all iPod models and iPod nanos have had photo capabilities. That extends not only to storing and viewing individual shots but also displaying your collection as a slide show and, in the case of the full-sized iPod, displaying your collection on a TV screen.

Preparing your photo collection

Before we look at some of these intriguing possibilities how do you get your image collection on to your iPod? Both the iPod and the iPod nano can synchronize with popular image organization and image manipulation programs. This includes:

- iPhoto: (Mac only) from version 4.0.3
- Adobe Photoshop Album (Windows)
- Adobe Photoshop Elements (Windows).

If your computer is not blessed with any of these applications there's no need to rush out and buy one: you can also point your iPod at any folders that you might use to store images downloaded from a digital camera. In the case of Windows PCs that might be your My Pictures folder; on the Macintosh it might be the iPhoto Library (in the Pictures folder) if you have a copy of iPhoto that is before version 4.0.3.

Digital image file formats

The iPod is rather picky about the audio file formats that you can load on it, but that's of little consequence because the music you import or purchase will already be in this format and fully

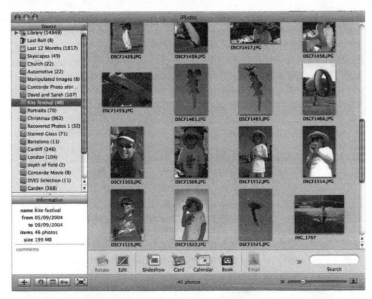

iPhoto: spot the family resemblance? iPhoto's library along with albums, can be downloaded to a compatible iPod.

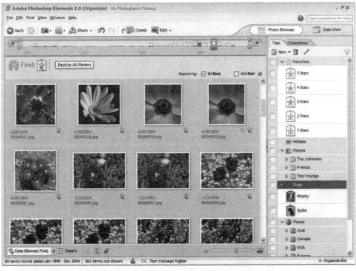

Photoshop Elements: if you save and manage your images in Photoshop Elements, your collection can easily be transferred to a supported iPod.

compatible. For image files it's quite likely that you have a wide range of different file types in your collection. Digital cameras, for example, normally output their images in JPEG or TIFF. If you're a fan of Photoshop and used it to enhance your photos you may well have some Photoshop files – in the PSD format. With this diversity in mind the iPod is compatible with a number of different file types.

- For Windows computers that compatibility amounts to the following types: JPEG, TIFF, PSD, BMP, GIF, SGI and PNG.

- On Macintosh computers the list is broadly similar: JPEG, TIFF, PSD, BMP, GIF, SGI, PNG, PICT and JPG2000.

If your photos are in one of these formats (and it'll be unusual if they are not) then you're all set to load them on your iPod.

Transferring photos to your iPod

When you are ready to copy your images to your iPod here's what you need to do:

1 Connect your iPod as you do when synchronizing with your music library.

2 Click on the **iPod** icon in the Sources window and then on the **Photos** tab.

3 Click the **Sync photos from** button and choose the location from which you want the photos downloaded. This may be an application or a folder (you have the option to choose a folder should you need to specify one you've created).

4 For some applications you can choose only to synchronize selected albums. Think of this rather like synchronizing only selected playlists; if you don't have the capacity to download a large image library this is a good way to transfer just the important images.

5 For the full-size iPod only, you can also choose to download the full-size, full-resolution copies of the photos. Click the **Include full-resolution photos** option if you wish to do this.

6 Click on **OK**.

7 If you have requested that full-resolution images are down-loaded you may want to click on **Enable disk use**, in the **Summary** pane (on the **Summary** tab). This will give you the

option of transferring your images to another computer, a feature avid digital photographers find particularly useful (we'll discuss this a little later).

8 Your images will be downloaded. If you have a large library and have selected the full-resolution images this may take some time. On future syncs this will all happen automatically and only changes to your library (such as newly downloaded images) will be transferred. Expect this to be much quicker.

As the download is in progress you'll get a message saying 'Optimizing Photos for iPod'. This is letting you know that iTunes, on behalf of your image library and iPod, is enhancing your images with respect to displaying them on the iPod screen and on TV. It does not modify the original image files, nor will it modify the full-resolution image files, if you've requested that they be copied as well.

Note that unlike music, where you can authorize several computers to provide tracks that can be exchanged, an iPod is linked to a single computer's image library. If you try to sync to another you'll find your original image collection is wiped.

Viewing your photo collection

How do you get to see the photos on your iPod? Go to the main iPod menu screen and select **Photos to display** in the **Photos** menu. Then you can select either Photo Library – if you want to scroll through your entire library or scroll down to a specific album (presuming that you downloaded albums when you last synced).

Whichever you select, you'll then be presented with a screen full of thumbnail images. Navigate through your collection in the following way:

♦ To jump to the next screen of thumbnails press the **Next** button on the click wheel.

♦ To jump to the previous screen press the **Previous** button.

♦ To select any image on a thumbnail page, spin the click wheel. The selected image will be highlighted in yellow.

♦ To view the selected image full screen, press the **centre** button.

♦ Press the **Menu** button to return to the thumbnail view.

Setting up a slideshow

Manually selecting individual images to display full screen is okay, but whether you want to enjoy them yourself, or share with friends or family, a collection of photos looks much better as a slideshow. Macintosh users familiar with iPhoto's slideshow feature will feel at home – the iPod slideshows are very similar.

Before running a show you'll need to configure the iPod. From the Photos menu select Slideshow Settings (see page 72). Here's how you can control your show:

- **Time Per Slide:** vary the time each photo appears.

- **Music:** choose a playlist for your background music. You can also choose not to have any music. Macintosh users who have also set up a slideshow with music in iPhoto have the additional option of selecting the iPhoto background music.

- **Repeat:** set this to 'on' and the show will repeat from the start after the final slide.

- **Shuffle Photos:** when 'on' photos are displayed randomly.

- **Transitions:** set a wipe, dissolve or other effect for the transition between slides (tip: simple ones work best).

- **TV Out:** set this to 'on' if you intend to display a slideshow on a TV screen. If you set it to 'ask' you'll be prompted each time as to where you want the show to be displayed. This option is not available on the iPod nano.

- **TV Signal:** the choice is PAL (for Europe, most of Africa, Asia and Australasia) or NTSC (the Americas and Japan).

Once you've made all your settings you can start the show by pressing the Play/Pause button on the click wheel. Your show will begin with the music you've requested and all the other settings you've configured. You can, at any point, jump ahead by a photo (or go back one) by pressing the Next and Previous buttons. If you interrupt the slideshow in this way it will pick up again from the currently selected image.

Replaying a slide show through a TV

You can connect your iPod to a television using special cable sets designed for the purpose or by using a Universal Dock. If you use a dock that features S-video connectors this will deliver a better image quality than the standard RCA/phono connectors. In either case, if you want sound along with your TV slide show you'll need to connect the audio RCA connectors to your TV: S-video cabling doesn't carry sound.

Also called phono leads, RCA connectors can connect most iPod docks with a TV. If your TV has a Scart connector you can purchase adaptors or leads that terminate with a Scart plug at one end.

With the connections established you can now configure your iPod for replay:

1   On your iPod select **Photo > Slideshow Settings > TV Out > On**. This will direct the output to the TV rather than the iPod's screen.

2   On the **Slideshow Settings** menu select the TV signal appropriate to the television set.

3   Turn on your TV and iPod. Depending on the television set you are using, the output from the iPod may automatically configure the television to replay the video signal or you may have to manually select a video input corresponding to the connection you are using.

4   If you are viewing on a widescreen TV you may need to change the format from widescreen to standard.

Transferring your photo collection to another computer

If you have stored your photos in a high-resolution format (that's exact copies of the original files) you can copy them to another computer. As these images are likely to be your own, there are none of the problems with regard to copyright that limit the way music files can be copied from iPod to computer.

To transfer your images you will need to have ensured that the **Enable Disk Use** option is selected (as we described above in the section *Transferring photos to your iPod*, page 107). When you connect your iPod to another computer you'll be able to see a folder within called **Photos**. You can then drag out the images you want to load to the new host computer.

iPods, iTunes and video

There's no mistaking the value of being able to carry a photo collection around with you. Arguably our photos contain more memories than our music and so it was a natural extension to the 'music-everywhere' concept to add photo capabilities to an iPod. However, it was the addition, a good year after photos, of video that had the greatest impact. Apple has confounded critics who said that a device with a viewing screen as small as the iPod would be too small to be of any use. The video iPod and the larger-screened iPhone have proved a massive success. Though they may not have invented a market for portable video, iPods have made that market largely their own: many video download services – not just iTunes – produce iPod compatible video.

Adding videos to your iTunes library

There are two ways you can add videos to your iTunes library: import them from any of the various sources (of which more later) or purchase them through the iTunes Store. At this point we're talking about video in a rather generic sense; video can comprise anything from a music video promo, episode of a TV show or even some digital video you've produced yourself.

Purchasing video from the iTunes Store

The process of purchasing video from the Store is just the same as that for music except, of course, you need to select the video

Videos from the iTunes Store: whether a music video, TV show or movie clip, you can download them all conveniently from the iTunes Store.

option on the iTunes Store home page. You can even preview a few seconds of many videos before committing to a purchase. You will have to wait a little longer for your downloads than for songs – video files are substantially larger than music ones.

Adding your own video

If you have your own video files – maybe you've downloaded one from a website or have some home movie footage – you can add it to your library by dragging the file's icon from your computer desktop to the iTunes main window. Alternatively, select **File > Add to Library** and then select the appropriate file.

Video formats

Videos available on the Web are produced, like image and music files, in a range of different formats. For them to be accepted by iTunes for inclusion in your library the video must be in either

QuickTime Pro: this modest application lets you convert most video formats into that accepted by iTunes.

QuickTime Movie or MPEG-4 formats. You can identify those files by their extensions which will be .mov, .mp4 or .m4v. If you have video that is in an alternate format you will need to convert it first. You can do this using freeware and shareware applications that are available on the Internet; or you can use Apple's QuickTime Pro. You'll have to pay (a modest) amount for this but it's quick and effective. You can then export your movie as an MPEG-4 file (preserving much of the original quality) or in an iPod format, optimized in file size and resolution for an iPod.

Converting video for the iPod

As well as converting video using applications such as QuickTime Pro, there are others that will produce iPod compatible video from a range of sources including DVDs. Some to check out include Roxio's Easy Media Creator suite (for Windows) and

X-OOM's Movies on PSP is designed to produce video for replay on Playstation Portables but will also produce files that are compatible with iTunes and iPods.

the same company's Toast (for Mac). There's also Intervideo's iVideoToGo.

The arrival of the iPod Touch and iPhone has increased interest in video conversions. Applications such as iPhone Video Converter (which despite the name can produce video for standard iPods) can convert file types including DivX, ASF, Rm, MOV, XviD, VOB, RMVB, FLV and MPG, to that which the iPod and iPhone can replay. This application can convert a batch of files (rather than one at a time) and transfer them to your device too.

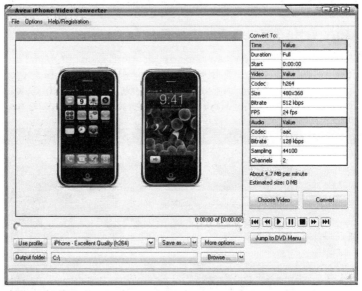

iPhone Video Converter: a simple application that produces video compatible with iPhone and any other video-compatible iPod.

Organizing your videos

You'll notice that the Source window in iTunes offers separate icons for movies and TV shows. There's also a smart playlist called Music Videos. Generally you'll find that any video you import will be filed away in the appropriate category. However, video you import yourself may be incorrectly assigned; if you want these to appear under the correct heading you'll need to modify some of the file information so that iTunes can correctly identify it.

To do this:

1 Select **File > Get Info** (or use the keyboard shortcuts of [**Control**]+[**I**] or [**Apple key**]+[**I**]).

2 Click on the **Video** option to open the **Video** pane.

3 Click on the **Video Kind** drop-down menu.

4 Select the appropriate video type: the options are Movie, TV Show and Music Video.

If you wish, you can also add additional information on this screen that will later help you locate and organize your videos.

Playing videos

Playing your videos in iTunes is just like playing your songs. Locate the respective video, click on it and enjoy. If you prefer to scan through your main library you'll see your videos listed along with your music tracks. A small, discrete icon – a symbolic TV screen adjacent to the track name – indicates which of the items in the list is a video.

You can choose to play your video:

◆ In the Album Artwork window (at the base of the Sources window)

◆ In a separate window

◆ Full screen.

You can choose between these three options by selecting **File > Preferences > General** and then, in the **Play videos** drop-down menu, make your selection. The **View** menu in iTunes also lets you choose what size window is displayed, from full screen through to half size.

It's worth pointing out that video can vary in its quality and resolution. In the early days of the iTunes Store, much of the video downloaded was sufficient only for iPod replay. View it full screen on your computer and, by virtue of the low resolution, it would look very poor. Nowadays higher and higher quality video material is available which looks much more impressive when displayed larger.

Video on your iPod

Of course, the reason that video was originally supplied at fairly low resolution was that it was intended to be viewed on an iPod. So how do you send your video collection to your iPod? Just the same way as your music and photos: automatically or manually.

For automatic transfers you need – the very first time you synchronize your movies – to click on your iPod's icon in the sources window and then on Movies. Make sure the Sync Movies check box is selected. Because you might want to sync movies to catch up with the latest episode of a TV series that you've missed, this pane also allows you to select which video matter is transferred. You may want all your videos on your iPod but it's more likely that you will want just selected ones. Video files are very large and you could quickly find that your iPod's capacity is reached.

Manually you can drag video titles from your library and drop them onto the iPod icon. Or you can create a video playlist (in exactly the same ways as a music one) and download this.

Playing video on your iPod

Once your video is downloaded to your iPod you can watch it.

1 From the main **iPod** menu (on the classic or third generation nano) select **Videos** (see page 71) and from that sub-menu select the category containing your chosen video. Each of these will take you to a further menu listing your options.

2 When you've made your selection press the **Play/Pause** button to start the replay. The same button will also let you pause your video should you need to and pick it up again later from the same point.

3 If you need, or want, to scroll through a video, tap the centre button briefly to call up a progress bar along the bottom of the screen. Spin the click wheel to fast forward or rewind your way through the video.

4 To move backwards and forwards at a slower speed you can hold the fast forward or rewind buttons on the click wheel. The movie will jump back or forwards in small increments in just the same way that you can move through an audio file.

You can play video on the iPod Touch by Coverflow selection.

Playing video on your TV

You can play your video on a TV by connecting it in just the same way as we described for viewing photo slideshows. You'll need to configure your iPod again, this time to output video:

1   On the iPod main menu select **Videos > Video Settings**.

2   Set **TV Out** to **On**.

3   Set **TV Signal** to **PAL** or **NTSC**, as appropriate.

4   Set **Widescreen** either on or off, according to the aspect ratio of the source material.

The quality you'll get will be surprisingly good for most videos that you can download today. Do be mindful of the comments earlier that some early video downloads were of slightly lower quality: these will still be quite watchable and the difference in quality will only be obvious when compared with more recent material.

Playing video on your TV using Apple TV

Extending the functionality of iTunes in the home is Apple TV. It makes the premise that you'd prefer to use your iPod for your music, pictures and video on the move and that you'd rather not have to connect up your iPod to a television at home every time you want to watch a video.

Apple TV is essentially a small set-top box, just like you'd use for cable, satellite or digital terrestrial television. Unlike these boxes it connects – wirelessly – to your computer (both Windows PCs and Macintoshes are supported) and enables you to stream video directly from your iTunes library to your TV.

In fact, Apple TV lets you stream anything from your iTunes library, not just movies. So, if you've a TV equipped with a first rate sound system, you can enjoy your audio collection too.

Beyond iTunes? The Apple TV system can also stream video from other Internet sources such as YouTube.

Apple TV lets you stream all the media from your iTunes collection direct to your television – wirelessly.

Summary

The great thing about the iTunes/iPod combo is that it can handle photos and video in pretty much the same way as music. And just as easily. You should now be clear that your iPod is not just a comprehensive music player but something much more. It can help you carry your photographic memories with your everywhere too; and let you catch up on that missed TV show or news summary on the way to the office in the morning. An iPod really can become the hub of your digital life.

Also, Apple TV, which we can regard as the home-based sibling of the iPod, can let you enjoy your music, photos and video on your large-screen TV as well.

By now you'll probably be wondering what else you can do with your iPod and iTunes. The answer is quite a lot and we'll discover some of these in Chapter 9. Next, though, we'll take a closer look at the podcasts and podcasting.

08

podcasting

In this chapter you will learn:

- about the nature of podcasts
- how to find and subscribe to podcasts
- how you can update podcasts
- how to create your own podcast

It's strange that although most iPod owners proudly display their device almost in the manner of a badge of honour, some people feel a little uneasy about ownership. All that money just to, self indulgently, enjoy a few songs, they might say. Of course, you or I might turn that around: so little money to enjoy so much music. On more than one occasion, however, it's been pointed out that iPods have an educational value too: you can use them to listen to, or watch, those informative things, podcasts. Okay, so not all podcasts are necessarily educational, at least in the accepted sense, but many people find them compelling and eagerly await each new episode. Here is a whole new rationale for owning an iPod!

In this chapter we'll take a look at what podcasts are, how you can find those of interest to you and how they can be delivered directly to your copy of iTunes (and hence, of course, to your iPod). We'll also take a look at how you can create your own podcasts and make them available via the iTunes Store.

What is a podcast?

Podcasts let anyone with a microphone, computer and an Internet connection publish audio (and video) broadcasts that can be listened to and subscribed to by any interested party who also has an Internet connection. Podcasts can comprise:

+ Full or condensed version of radio shows

+ News and current affairs programming

+ Audio books issued in instalments

+ Specialized business and technology news programming

+ Music news

+ Corporate news and information.

In fact, any material that would benefit from the episodic release – and which some people would be interested in – may be worth producing as a podcast.

Unlike conventional downloads – such as songs or audio books – podcasts tend to be episodic: there may be a weekly or even daily release of a new episode. You can access these episodes by subscribing, either at a website hosted by the creator of the podcasts (the podcaster) or via an aggregation system which will check websites for new episodes and downloading, ready for you to review. I won't go into the technicalities of aggregation here because there's no need. Why? Because iTunes is – amongst other things – an aggregator, and will provide all the necessary services with the minimum instruction or intervention on your part. So iTunes will download all your selected podcasts automatically. And that selection might also include the video version of the podcast (a vodcast or video podcast) that can later be viewed on a video compatible iPod.

Searching for podcasts

There are thousands of free podcasts available through iTunes. Though many podcasters can provide direct access to their podcasts via their own website, most now realize that iTunes is most people's first port of call when searching for those on their favourite subjects.

* To find them, select the iTunes Store from iTunes' Sources window and click on Podcasts.

Finding podcasts: to find any podcasts begin by selecting the iTunes Store and selecting Podcasts.

When you select the podcasts option from the iTunes Store homepage you'll see a page very similar to that of the main store – except this time every category relates to podcasts. You can browse new releases, featured video podcasts, staff favourites, what's hot or the podcast charts.

If you are looking for a specific category then you can select on from a listing, or if you know that something you are looking for comes from a specific provider (such as the BBC or, say, Reuters) you can search by publisher. Select a category and it will bring up a new page featuring popular podcasts on that subject along with any new or recent headlining podcasts. You'll also see, for most categories, a list of sub-categories to allow you to refine your search.

Downloading podcasts

Once you've found a selection of podcasts on a subject you're interested in, you'll probably be amazed by the number: even some abstract and niche subject areas can boast a large number of podcasts. When you see them listed, there's not much information about them, generally just a 'Subscribe' button. Unless you have found exactly what you are looking for it's a good idea not to click on this; instead click on the name of the podcasts.

This will bring you to a new page that provides more descriptive information about the podcast and, rather like the page devoted to your favourite artist's latest album, gives a list of all the 'tracks' available. In fact, this is not a list of tracks but rather a list of episodes. Rather than subscribing to the whole series you might like to just download those episodes on topics that you are especially interested in. Or you can download a single episode to see if it covers the material you expect. Only then – when you've okayed the material – would you subscribe.

Actually there are many more podcasts than are listed up front in the iTunes Store. You can download any of these others – via iTunes – if you know where on the Internet iTunes can go to find them. To do so, you'll need to know the URL of the podcast. You can find this out from the publisher of the podcast and it's usually available via the publisher's own website.

* To subscribe to these independent podcasts select the **Advanced > Subscribe to Podcast**. You will then need to paste the URL into the dialogue box that appears.

When an individual podcast has been downloaded, or you've subscribed and the latest edition has been downloaded, you can find it by selecting the Podcasts icon in the iTunes Sources window. This will display a list of the podcasts you've downloaded. Those to which you have subscribed will appear listed by title. If you've not listened to (or viewed) any, there will be a small indicator to the left of the title. Click on the adjacent triangle to see a full listing of all episodes.

If you've downloaded discrete episodes of some podcasts, these will be listed along with a **Subscribe** button. This serves the same purpose as the Subscribe button in the iTunes Store listing. Click on this to begin subscribing to the chosen podcast.

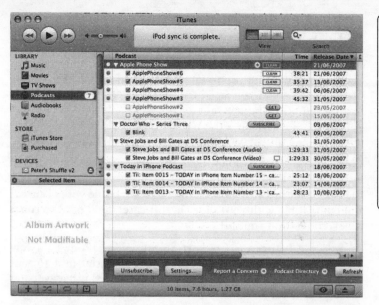

Podcast window: click on the Podcast icon in the sources window to reveal the podcasts. The spot in column one indicates those podcasts that have not been viewed or listened to. You can unsubscribe using the button at the bottom of the screen.

Unsubscribing from podcasts

Podcast episodes will be downloaded continuously until you want them to stop. To do this you need to unsubscribe.

1 Select the **Podcast** icon in the Sources window and highlight the podcast you want to unsubscribe from in the listing.

2 Click on the **Unsubscribe** button at the bottom of the page.

3 When you unsubscribe, any editions of the podcast already downloaded will remain on your computer; if you want to delete these too, press [**Delete**] immediately after clicking the **Unsubscribe** button.

Podcast practicalities

Do you need an iPod to enjoy podcasts? No. Just like music and video you can enjoy your favourite podcasts directly on your computer. You can play them from within iTunes just like any other media. If it's a video podcast you can even relay it to your television using Apple TV (page 117). In fact, and Apple don't make a big song and dance about this, you don't even need an iTunes account to download podcasts. You will only need an account if you create your own podcasts and submit them to the Store.

Got a podcast that doesn't play? If you've acquired podcasts from a variety of sources, from within iTunes and elsewhere, you may find that some don't play on your iPod. That's because iTunes is more lax with podcasts than it is with music in regard to the format that they are supplied in. They may be supplied by the podcaster in a format that, though compatible with iTunes is not compatible with your iPod. In this case you'll need to run a quick conversion routine:

* Select **Advanced > Convert Selection for iPod**. In a few moments iTunes will re-encode your material in a format acceptable to your iPod. You can then copy this new version to your iPod.

Note that podcasts can also be included in playlists but if you do that, new episodes are not added automatically.

Create your own podcasts

If you really enjoy getting and sharing information from podcasts why not consider creating your own? It's not as difficult as you might think. These are the key steps involved:

1 Gather together the elements of your prospective podcast and produce a script.

2 Record your podcast.

3 Edit your raw recordings.

4 Publish your polished recording to allow others to subscribe.

5 Promote your production so potential subscribers know to subscribe.

Let's look at these steps in a little more detail. You don't have to use any special software but doing so – using software applications dedicated to podcasting – can make the task a whole lot simpler. A great example of one that can help you through the entire process is Podium by Softease (**www.softease.co.uk**). That's the product we've used to create the podcast described below.

Preparing your podcast

Begin by getting together all the material you want to use for your podcast. You'll need a microphone that will work with your computer. Nothing too complex or expensive: a simple microphone will be fine and if it comes with a table mount or tripod, so much the better; that will allow you more freedom when recording.

Write out a rough script. Because there is so much choice in podcasts, if you want yours to stand out from the crowd – or even be considered on a par with others – it needs to be well structured and well presented. Once you've got a rough idea of what you want to say it's time to start up the software.

In Podium, begin by selecting Create a new project. Then:

1 Fill in the podcast details: enter the name of the podcast, your name as the author and, optionally, a podcast description. This information will be used later when you publish your podcast.

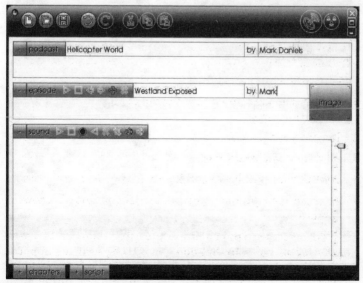

Podium: filling in the initial details to identify the podcast.

2 Fill in the episode details: this will be the details of the specific episode you are about to record. If you wish, you can include an image here. Images will be displayed when you make the episode available on the Internet.

3 Open the script workspace: Podium lets you create and build your script within the application itself. It allows you to create a multi-speaker script where each of the speakers in your production (if there is more than one) has their own parts clearly defined. This is ideal if you are into amateur dramatics and want to publish your latest production (or excerpts thereof) with a cast of players.

You can now type in your script. If you have roughed out something in another application (such as Word) you can cut and paste your text from that document into the script window.

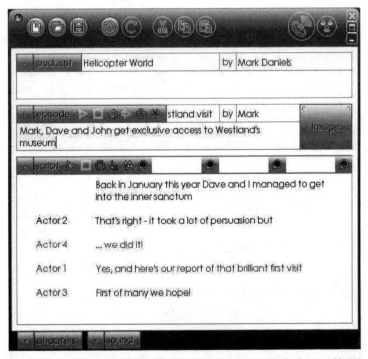

Scripting a podcast: podcasting applications allow you to script a single or multi-part podcast. Details entered in the Podcast and Episode windows will be displayed in iTunes.

Rehearsing the script

Just like any professional production you'll get the best results if you rehearse. And rehearse again. Often, experienced podcasters will tell you, your first script may look good but when you read it aloud it just doesn't flow well. That's why it pays to read it out several times and, if there are any cumbersome words or phrases, re-write them. Make sure your script matches your reading style rather than your writing; in that way it will be more natural for you to read and sound more natural as part of your podcast.

You can use the software to rehearse and practise the speed and timings – particularly important if you have a podcast involving several people. In Podium, click on the Play button in the Script toolbar. Rather like a television autocue the text will be highlighted line by line and you can move through at an appropriate speed. You can also print off a copy of the script if you want to practise away from the computer.

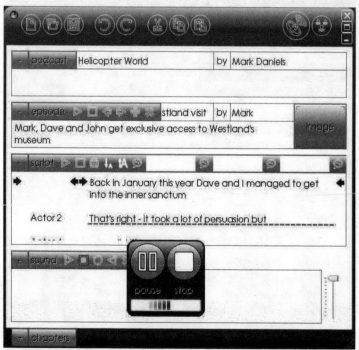

Recording a script: when you record your script, the lines you need to read are underlined as you read them. You can move from line to line by hitting the space bar.

Recording your audio

When you are totally happy with your words and your diction, you can record your audio for real.

1 Start recording by clicking the **Record** button. You'll be given a 3... 2... 1... countdown then recording will begin. There's a terrible urge in us all, when recording, to forget all that rehearsing and rush headlong into reading the script. Take your time. Read at a steady pace and follow the cues on the script screen.

2 At the end of the script, pause for a second or two and then press the **Stop** button. You'll see a waveform, representing the voice, appear on the screen. If there has been more than one person involved in the recording you'll see each person's

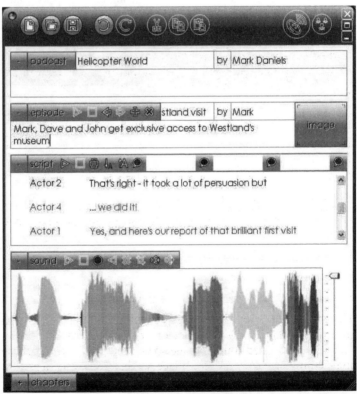

Audio waveform: at the end of the recording you will see the waveform of the audio. Parts spoken by different people are indicated in different colours.

part of the waveform represented in a different colour. What you need to ensure (to have a recording where all the voices are at the same volume) is that the amplitude of the waveform (the vertical height) is, on average, similar throughout.

3 Use the **Play** button now to play back the recording. Many of us don't like hearing our own voice replayed – if that's the case with you, have someone else listen too so that you can get a more objective opinion of the recording.

4 First time through don't be surprised if you pick up on a number of mistakes and fluffs. Don't worry – we all make them. Just delete the recording and have another go.

Editing your audio track

Sometimes you'll end up with a generally good recording but there will be odd noises, pauses and gaps. Perhaps the microphone has picked up that sharp intake of breath at the start or a muffled cough half way through. That's no cause to discard the whole recording. You can use the editing tools provided in the software to reduce the replay volume over these sections.

If you are familiar with the editing tools provided with digital video software you'll immediately recognize the similar tools provided for the audio editing.

These let you:

• Select a section of the audio

• Delete a section of the audio

• Crop the audio (that is, select a portion of the audio and delete the rest)

• Insert new audio into an existing audio track

• Replace a section of audio

• Alter the volume of a section of the audio.

These tools allow you tremendous freedom to re-engineer your recordings to make them as close to perfect as possible. However, as all seasoned sound engineers will tell you, it makes sense to get things right in the first place so that editing is kept to a minimum!

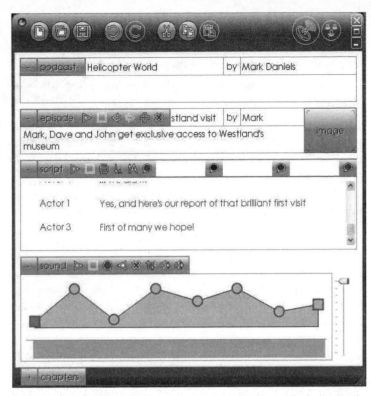

Audio editing: you can modify the audio track by changing the amplitude (to alter the levels) and adding a second track.

The editing tools also let you add an additional soundtrack. This might be used for background music, for example. You can also use the editing tools to modify this track so that it works well with the main audio track.

Publishing your podcast

By publishing your podcast, we mean making it available for anyone who wants to hear it to do so; that generally involves loading it on a server somewhere on the Internet to which there is public access.

In Podium you begin the publishing process by clicking on the Publish button. You will have previously configured the program so that it can upload your podcasts to an appropriate place on the Internet. In case you don't have any webspace of your own that you can use, Podium provides some, along with all the information that you need to specify to enable others to listen to your podcast.

Promoting your podcast

When you publish your podcast it's available on the Web but, if no one knows about it you'll have no one visiting and subscribing. You need to publicize it to generate interest and visitors.

Click on the **Promote** button to start the process – this will let you share the unique URL address of your podcast (that visitors will need to use to subscribe) through e-mail or documents.

This will give you limited exposure, perhaps to your e-mail list or your address book. If you want a wider audience to have the chance to enjoy your efforts you can submit your production to Apple and iTunes. To submit your production you need to launch iTunes, go to the iTunes Store and click on the **Podcasts** link. On the **Learn More** box, click on the **Submit a Podcast** link. This will provide you with all the instructions for submitting a podcast.

Submit to iTunes: select Podcast from the iTunes Store home page and you'll find the Submit Podcast button. Click on this to make your submission.

Once you've made a submission your podcast goes into a queue where it will await review by a member of the iTunes podcasting staff. You will, when it reaches the top of the queue, hear whether it has been accepted or rejected. If it's been rejected don't get too despondent. There are a number of reasons that Apple cite:

- Technical problems: this is something that's easy to check and correct. If your links don't work and the iTunes guys can't access it they will have to dismiss it out of hand; they won't be able to fix any problems for you, no matter how trivial (though this problem is usually diagnosed as part of the original submission process).

- Requirement of a login or password to access the feed or any episodes. Again, if people can't easily get into the system you'll be rejected.

- Explicit language in the title or description: there's no ban on explicit material in the content of a podcast (which can be hidden from general view by use of tags and parental controls) but there should not be any in the title or description – which can be viewed by anyone.

Rejection: iTunes will prequalify details of your podcast, such as valid URLs, before your final submission to avoid delays in the process.

- Strong sexual content: it's not specified by Apple what this is precisely, but good taste rules apply.

- Apparent misuse of copyrighted material: Apple need to be assured that there are no copyright violations – if you've used (quite innocently) some background music that could be considered to be copyright and you don't clearly have permission to use it, your podcast can be rejected.

It should go without saying that offensive material of any sort will result in rejection.

If you have been rejected, that's only on the basis of the original submission. If you have fallen foul of one of the rejection criteria, you can correct the problem (or contentious elements) and resubmit. You can also visit the iTunes Help and Apple website for more information on getting your submissions passed.

Once you have been passed, what happens next? Your podcast will appear in iTunes Search and shortly afterwards in iTunes Browse categories. There are no promises on how long this takes but it's normally around a week.

Summary

There's no doubt that podcasts are an important resource in iTunes and becoming increasingly more so. You'll only discover the breadth of the material when you start exploring. If you don't find something that's useful to you, you should now realize that it's possible to create your own professional grade podcasts. All it takes is the right software and just a little practice.

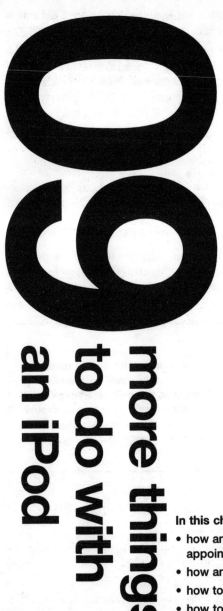

09

more things to do with an iPod

In this chapter you will learn:

- how an iPod can keep your appointments
- how an iPod can help you get fit
- how to make an iPod into a PDA
- how to store camera images
- how to back up your files
- how to avoid getting lost

Okay, it may be a bit excessive to describe an iPod as a mini computer: there may be a lot of things it can do just as well as a mini computer, but there are a great number of things it can't. It's just that, with regard to what it does, it does very well. We've seen how effectively it lets you enjoy your music collection, show off your photos and even keep up to date with your favourite TV shows.

In this chapter we take a look as some of the less obvious things that you can use your iPod for. They may not be as profound as those we've already discussed but they might just prove a lifesaver – in a digital sense – when you are out and about.

Keep in touch, keep alert: contacts and calendars

If you are fortunate to have one of those touch-sensitive iPods – an iPhone – then you've a great diary and address book built in as standard. But did you realize that even a standard iPod can handle both your contact details and calendar? Here's how.

A calendar on your iPod

If you are a Windows Microsoft Outlook user or a Macintosh iCal user then you'll be able to take your diary with you everywhere, and keep it up to date every time you synchronize with your computer.

To enable your iPod for calendar syncing for the first time:

1 Connect your iPod to your computer.

2 Select the iPod icon from the Sources window.

3 When the iPod screen is displayed in the main window, click on the **Contacts** tab.

4 Click the **Sync** button at the top of the screen. This will say 'Sync calendars from Microsoft Outlook' or 'Sync iCal calendars' according to your operating system.

5 If you have more than one calendar you can choose which one to sync (you might want to synchronize only your personal calendar, or your work one) or you can sync them all.

6 Click the **Apply** button.

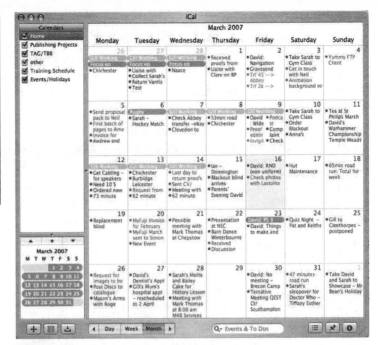

Calendars: many iPods – including some pre-colour models can sync with computer based calendars.

Your iPod should now start to update by adding in all the new calendar information. Once done, disconnect your iPod and check the information: select **iPod > Extras > Calendars.** If there's more than one calendar, select one (you can only view one at a time) and press the centre button to view it.

Your calendar will be displayed, one month at a time with the month and year on show displayed in the screen banner. Any days that feature events will be indicated by a small flag icon. Use the scroll wheel to locate the day you wish to view and press the centre button again. You'll see the day in question along with details of the events on that day.

If you've programmed alerts in your computer-based calendar, you may be pleased (or not) to know that these have been transferred to your iPod too. If you want to turn these off (or on, having removed them) select **iPod > Extras > Calendars > Alarms.** This gives you the choice of 'Off', 'Beep' or 'Silent'.

Keep your contacts with you

Adding your computer's address book to your iPod involves a similar process to the calendar (in fact, as you've probably noticed, the method of setting up any new features such as these begins in much the same way):

1 Connect the iPod to your computer.

2 Select the **iPod** icon from the Sources window.

3 Click on the **Contacts** tab (as you did for syncing with the calendar).

4 Click on the **Sync** button. On a Windows PC you'll be given the question **Sync contacts from** and a choice of different options in the pull-down menu (normally Microsoft Outlook or the default Windows address book).

   Macintosh users will have the single option of **Sync Address Book contacts**.

5 Click on the **Apply** button to apply the changes.

To allow syncing with an iPod you'll need to ensure that, as a Windows user, you've stored your contacts in Outlook 2003 (or later), Outlook Express, or Windows Address Book. The latter is the listing that Outlook uses to access contact information, but is also available on computers that do not have Outlook installed.

Macintosh users will need to ensure that they are running OS X Tiger (10.4) or later and are using the OS X Address Book. If you have Microsoft Office installed, note that Entourage is not supported.

Now whenever you modify your contact list on your computer, the changes will also be made on the copy in your iPod. That applies to both additions and deletions.

Finding contacts

To find a contact, start from the iPod main menu and select **Extras > Contacts**. You can then use the scroll wheel to scan through your contacts and the centre button to display the chosen one.

Keep fit with your iPod

The iPod – in all its guises – has become almost obligatory amongst the running and jogging fraternity. Though a few of the most dedicated persevered in the past with tape and CD-based music systems, neither was ideal for active sports: tape machines were bulky and had limited capacity; CD players were a little more convenient but we prone to skipping and interruptions. CD mechanisms were just not built for use on the go.

Fitness and your iPod

All iPods boast a resistance to shock – so your music will play on no matter how much exertion your training regime puts you through. Even a full-size iPod is pretty lightweight to carry with you, though iPod nanos and shuffles are even more so. The shuffle can easily be pinned, using the supplied clip, to a shirt or pocket – while others can be kept safe using custom sports cases and bands. Kitted out, you can set out on your run or gym work with your favourite tracks playing to stave off the boredom.

For a little inspiration you could even turn to the iTunes podcasts: look under **Categories > Health** and you'll find a number of podcasts dedicated to health and fitness. Download some and listen to them prior to, or during, your next activity.

The ultimate runner's solution

With the public interest in video and the anticipated iPhone, you could have been excused for missing the release – in the summer of 2006 – of the ultimate runner's iPod companion: the Nike+ iPod Sport Kit. This low-priced kit has two components: a sensor and a receiver. The receiver plugs into your iPod nano's dock connector and discretely adds a new Nike+ iPod option into the nano's menu.

The sensor fits to your running shoe and tracks your speed and distance. You could invest in some special Nike running shoes that have a secret compartment to conceal your sensor (several models are now compatible) or fix the sensor to your standard shoes – essential for those that struggle to find the ideal runners.

Nike+ iPod Sport Kit: with a discrete sensor slipped in a running shoe, the Sport Kit is an ideal way to both enjoy your music when running and monitor your performance.

When you're ready to take your first monitored run select the Nike+ iPod option from the menu and enter your weight. You can also specify whether your progress is to be measured in metric or imperial units, and whether you want audible feedback presented by a male or female voice. You can also designate one of your music tracks as a powersong: when you are flagging you can hit the iPod's centre button and have this uplifting track help give you a blast.

Finally, select what kind of a workout you want to do: choose from a basic run, distance based, time based or calorie burn. Apart from the basic mode, each will let you select a goal. No matter how ambitious, when you set a goal your iPod will advise you as to how close you are and how you are progressing. You can get additional support and information when you return home – not only will your iPod give you a full readout of the information gathered it will, next time you sync with your computer, send your performance information to the Nike website. There you can monitor your ongoing progress and produce reports that illustrate your improvement. You can even use the website to design new running routes.

How do you get the best from the kit? Here's some advice from a seasoned runner who's been using the iPod almost since it first arrived:

1 **Set goals:** it can be easy to procrastinate – if that's a valid term for the hard work of jogging – and not set any objectives.

It's been shown time and time again that by setting goals you'll achieve better and better results. That may be improvements to your time or extending your endurance. Take a look on the Nike website for some useful tips on setting and monitoring goals.

2 **Calibrate:** straight out of the box the Nike kit is remarkably good at monitoring your performance – certainly far more so than conventional pedometers. However they can still be out by as much as 5%. That may not sound too much but when you are after accuracy every percentage point matters. You can calibrate your kit by using a measured mile or even an athletics track. Again, details are available on the website.

3 **Monitor your progress:** you can press the centre button of your iPod and get instant audio feedback on your pace, along with instantaneous time and distance. Use this to check on how your pace changes with distance or even geography. When you get home you can get more details of your performance – and progress – at the Nike+ website.

4 **Create playlists for your running:** an ideal playlist will feature a mix of fast-paced music and more gentle-paced tracks. Depending on your running style you might alternate between the two, use two fast tracks followed by one slow. The faster your normal, or intended, pace the greater the proportion of fast-paced music you should build into your playlist. Don't forget a powersong – the song that will play if you press and hold the centre button. If this is a strong, up-tempo track it will give your running a boost, just when you need it.

5 **Compare notes:** the Nike kit can let you join a community of runners all around the world. You can use the community to help with your motivation or to set up intercontinental competitions where you can compete against others with a similar ability.

Create an iPDA

Unlike the iPod, which seems to be (almost) universally loved, there's something of a love–hate approach to PDAs – personal digital assistants. Some people love them and (like the keen iPod owner) would never leave home without them. Others view them less favourably.

Whatever your opinion on them, there's no denying that they do offer a range of tools that can make your day-to-day life simpler. Pukka PDAs offer access to your personal data, such as calendars, contacts, appointments and e-mail along with the ability to handle office documents.

Some of these functions, as we have seen, are easily supported by your iPod. What if you could add the others too? You may not have been able to justify (or want) a PDA, but if you could add the functionality to your existing iPod at a steal of a price, would that make more sense? If so, here's just one utility that makes this possible.

ZappTek's iPDA is built for Mac OS X (10.3 or later) and gives you all this PDA-style information:

• Transfer all (or some) of your Entourage events, contacts, messages, notes and tasks.

iPDA: the main screen of iPDA allows you to select which information is synced with your iPod.

- Transfer all (or some) of the information in your mail messages, address book contacts, iCal calendars and even Stickies.

- Transfer Google calendars (and any other web-based calendars that support the iCal standard).

- Back up files and folders from your computer to your iPod, ensuring all are backed up to the most recent versions.

- Transfer popular file formats including Acrobat PDFs, Microsoft Word (and RTF and text files) and Apple Pages documents.

- Download any RSS feeds (all those news stories that are automatically downloaded to your web browser).

- Download weather forecast information, driving directions and news/information.

For those that might be bemoaning the fact that calendars transferred to your iPod in the way described above lacked some information – such as events, flagged contacts, info on flagged or unflagged messages and tasks, you'll be pleased to hear that iPDA will successfully transfer all this information.

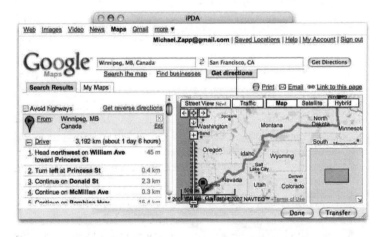

iPDA shows you the way: the iPDA software gives you direct access to Google maps to plan your journey – and transfer the instructions to your iPod.

Your iPod as a portable hard drive

When the first iPod appeared, those reviewers not sold on its virtues commented that it was merely a portable hard drive with a bit of software and a few controls added. Of course, they were right. Those iPods – and their descendants – are built around a portable hard drive although it's a bit dismissive of the technology that makes it an iPod to describe it as 'merely' a hard drive.

However, the fact that there is a hard disc at the core of your iPod (and a fair bit of flash memory in the nano, touch and shuffle) means you can use it in this guise to transport documents from computer to computer or even keep an extra backup of some important files.

To set up your iPod to give you access to its hard disc:

1 Attach your iPod to your computer.

2 Select the **iPod** from the Source window and then click on the **Summary** tab.

3 In the **Options** section, click the button marked **Enable Disk Use**.

4 Select **Apply** to apply the change.

If you are using an iPod shuffle you can, at step 3 above, use the onscreen slider to define how much of the memory you want to devote to your hard disc space.

Despite the iPod being compatible with Macintoshes and Windows PCs, there is one place where this falls down, and that's due to a shortcoming of Windows. Though a Macintosh can read the hard disc of an iPod formatted by a Windows computer, the reverse is not true. If you plan to share documents using your iPod make sure you set up the hard disc feature by connecting it first to the Windows PC and set it up there. It will then work fine with any Mac.

Once you've set up your iPod as a computer hard disc, it will behave just like one too. That means that the next time you sync, the iPod will appear on the Macintosh desktop or, for Windows PCs, in the My Computer window. You can open it in the same way as any other disc, open folders, copy files to and from it.

There are just a couple of points you must heed:

• Don't disconnect your iPod now without hitting the Eject button (the small icon next to the iPod's name in the Source window). Just like standard portable discs, you must tell the computer – by selecting Eject – that you want to remove it.

• Don't delete – or interfere – with folders called *Calendars*, *Contacts* or *Photos*. These contain information that your iPod needs to work correctly.

A companion for your digital camera

By now you'll be aware of, if not familiar with, the iPod's digital photo capabilities. But there's another string to its proverbial bow: you can use it to download images directly from a digital camera's memory card. Why might you want to do this? Well, if you're away on holiday and you've found you've shot enough photos to fill your camera's memory card – or cards, you either need to dump some images or copy them elsewhere. In the case of the latter, that's where your iPod comes in. On the basis that you are more likely to carry an iPod away on holiday or extended trip than your laptop, you can equip yourself with a modest camera adaptor that will let you download images from your camera's memory card.

To download your images all you need do is connect the camera adaptor to the iPod's dock (it works with all full-sized iPods from the iPod Photo onwards) and connect the camera's USB lead between it and the camera. With both devices switched on you can quickly transfer images across to the iPod, freeing your memory card for some more intensive shooting.

Maps, mapping and travel

After iPods and, perhaps, digital cameras, in-car navigation systems have been the big sellers of recent years. Simple, and ruthlessly efficient (if we forgive the odd wrong turn that sent granny into a stock car race…) they are a possible antidote for increasingly congested roads. What happens when you get out of the car though? Or you make a journey on foot, or by public transport? It's the iPod to the rescue again! Mindful that an iPod is a device that we carry with us everywhere, a number of software publishers – including Zapptek (creators of iPDA, as we saw above) have realized the potential of the iPod as a navigational and informational tool. Here's just a small sample of what's available and how you can enjoy the resources offered on your iPod.

Going underground

Suburban rail, underground and metro systems are something of a gift for iPod colour displays. You can easily store a whole continent's worth of rail maps in the space of a handful of images. If you want to add these maps to your iPod pay a visit to www.iSubwayMaps.com. Here you'll find a growing number of the world's transport systems all ready to download. It's a growing collection too, with special versions for 4G, 5G, classic and nano iPods. It's a simple installation – download a zipped file of images to your computer and then, in the same way that you might have synced an album of images to your computer, sync your iPod with the folder you've just downloaded. Full instructions are given on the website, as the details do vary according to the iPod model you are loading to.

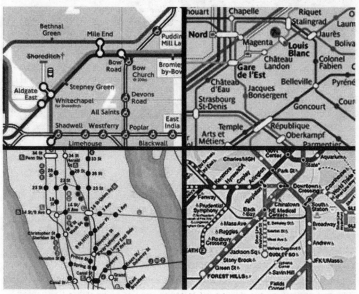

London, Paris, New York, Boston: thanks to iSubwayMaps.com you need never lose your way around any of the world's major cities.

It should go without saying that travelling a public transport system can make you vulnerable to theft – especially if you betray your iPod by courtesy of its iconic white earphones.

Eat, drink and be merry

If you're a fan of the Rough Guides to travelling you'll be pleased to hear that there's a version of their city guides that can be downloaded to your iPod. As part of an expanding range they currently offer eating and drinking guides for a number of the most popular tourist destinations that you can download to your iPod free of charge. They are compatible with all colour-screen iPods.

These guides are presented in the form of podscrolls – a series of screens, rather like a compact version of a PowerPoint presentation. You can make your way through them by spinning the click wheel. To load one onto your iPod you need only download a zipped file and follow the instructions included with the podscroll file.

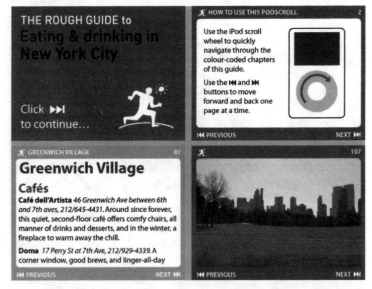

Podscrolls: simple but efficient, the podscrolls of the Rough Guides are a great way to find your way around the eateries and watering holes of major cities.

Enjoy YouTube on your iPod Touch and iPhone

If you're an iPod Touch or iPhone user, some of the features we've described above as extras will be available as standard on your enhanced iPod. For example, the calendar is automatically installed and configured. And on the iPhone you can also receive rich HTML emails – ones rich in graphics – as a matter of course.

Here's a bonus feature for the iPod Touch or iPhone user to enjoy: watch YouTube videos. These models have a special YouTube player that accesses content on the YouTube website and presents it on screen. Better still, when you find that intriguing video you just have to share, you can – iPhone will, at your command, create an email to send to friends that will automatically send them the correct YouTube link.

Summary

So, your iPod is proving to be a very capable device, one whose ultimate abilities seems to be limited only by the imaginations of those (largely third-party) programmers who create the applications we've discussed here. We're not suggesting that you must download all – or any – of the extra features we've described but, if nothing else, they demonstrate the capabilities of the ostensibly simple iPod.

The good news – for those hungry for even more – is that the burgeoning iPod industry shows no signs of slowing down. Sadly we don't have space here to discuss more, but you'll find some web addresses to explore in Chapter 11 on resources.

10

troubleshooting

In this chapter you will learn:

- what to do when your iPod begins acting irrationally
- about the special tools available to Windows users of iTunes
- about the iPod error symbols
- what to do when your iPod's battery starts to fail

This is one chapter in this book that I hope you don't *have* to read. But think of it like insurance. You don't want to have it, but if (and it is a really big if) something should go wrong, it's nice to know you've got it! Why don't I want you to read it? It's because it deals with rescuing your iPod in the face of potential problems.

The iPod is a remarkable device – but then you've probably discovered that already. However, like all devices there may be times when things are not quite right; strange logos and symbols appear and the iPod doesn't operate quite as expected. Very rarely this is due to a serious problem, one that only an authorized service centre can correct but usually (and we're still talking about rare events) it's something you can fix yourself. So, what can go wrong and how do you put it right?

The five 'R's of troubleshooting

Apple themselves have come up with a simple course of action to follow if you ever encounter a problem: they call it the 'Five 'R's': Reset, Retry, Restart, Reinstall, Restore and this is briefly what each involves:

Reset: the equivalent of a soft boot on a computer; think of it as the iPod's version of the [Control]-[Alt]-[Delete] command. We'll take a look at the process of resetting in a moment.

Retry: a system test that involves connecting the iPod into a different USB or FireWire port on your computer, or even one on another computer.

Restart: an action for your computer, it double checks the software on your computer and unties any knots there might be at that end; at this stage you can also check for any software updates, for iTunes or your iPod.

Reinstall: refresh your version of iTunes and the software on your iPod with the latest versions.

Restore: so far as your iPod is concerned, the last resort, a solution that restores your device to the condition it was in when it left the factory.

We should pre-empt a more thorough discussion of troubleshooting techniques with a cautionary warning. Service centres report a large number of iPods being returned with no problem at all. Why? Users had used the 'hold' switch on the top. With the iPod totally unresponsive they had feared the worst; simply sliding the switch to its unlocked position would have resumed the service as normal but, pessimists that we sometimes are, we err on the side of total failure. It's the sort of obvious mistake we can all laugh at but all fall victim to now and again!

Step 1: Reset

Resetting is a bit like a kick start; something to allow your iPod to quickly recover from whatever tangle it has got itself into.

To reset a full-sized iPod, nano or mini you need do the following. We're working on the presumption here that you've moved the hold slider to the unlocked position and that the batteries are fully charged (flat batteries probably come a close second to the hold switch as the actual cause of a presumed breakdown).

1 Press and hold the centre button and the Menu button simultaneously until you see the Apple logo appear on screen. This may take five or six seconds, or longer, but when the logo appears wait for the iPod to go through its restarting sequence.

2 At the end you should see the iPod main menu. Success! Your iPod should be back in step with itself and happy to obey your next commands.

Resetting an iPod shuffle is easier still: turn it off for a few seconds, then turn it on. The iPod shuffle is a simple beast and this simple solution should sort it.

No luck? Try connecting your iPod into a live power adaptor or to the dock (or cable) connected to your computer; the computer should be on and not asleep or hibernating.

Step 2: Retry

Sometimes, for no adequately explored reason, USB and FireWire connections can prove a little problematic. You might have seen this if you use an external hard drive. Nine times out of ten, when you start the computer, the drive appears on your desktop or in the My Computer folder. On the tenth attempt – no sign of it. You've changed no settings and done nothing unusual. Start again and it appears. So it can be with your iPod. Trying a different connection (on the same computer and, if you want to be doubly sure, on another) will help find any 'funnies' with your connections.

Step 3: Restart

Like your computer connections, software itself can sometimes be a bit unpredictable. It may, for example, not recognize your iPod when you plug it in, but restart the software and there it is, sitting innocently in your Sources window. Make sure too that your operating system software is fully up to date. Often the small updates that are periodically downloaded (or offered for download) may contain patches for known problems. Installing these updates might solve your iPod problem.

Step 4: Reinstall

Occasionally with all software-based applications there can be a glitch that damages its operation. Cunning error correction systems and auto repairing applications mean that these happen very infrequently, but when the software does get corrupted the only solution may be to reinstall.

To reinstall the software for your iTunes and iPod system:

1 Visit www.apple.com/itunes to download the latest version of iTunes.

2 Follow the on-screen instructions to install this software. If you are prompted to either Repair or Remove the existing software, try Repair first. This is quicker than a full reinstall.

3 Connect your iPod and click on its icon in the Sources window.

4 Check for the latest version of the iPod software.

Step 5: Restore

By which Apple means restoring your iPod to the factory settings. Sometimes – and very rarely – your iPod will become so confused that the only way to get it working normally again is to restore it to its original, factory settings. It's something of a drastic step and one that you need to distinguish from a mere software update.

When updates to your iPod's software are released and installed on your iPod you can think of them as being similar to updates to your computer's operating system. They add extra features, improve operation or fix problems with the current system. The files and data on your device (in the case of the iPod, the songs, video and other personal information) are not affected.

When you restore an iPod to its factory settings you're returning it to the condition it was when it first left the factory – and you unpacked it for the first time. Obviously, this means all the data and music you installed on it is gone. However, when you next synchronize your iPod (after setting it up again) all the music, video and everything else previously on your iPod will be recopied.

If you need to restore to factory settings, here's what you need to do:

1 Make sure you have the latest versions of iTunes loaded on your computer.

2 Open iTunes (after upgrading, if necessary) and connect your iPod using the standard cable you use to synchronize.

3 When the iPod appears in iTunes' Sources window, select it and click on the **Summary** tab in the main iTunes window.

4 Click on the **Restore** button. You'll see one of four different options.

   ◆ Option 1: Restore – restores the iPod using the iPod software already on the iPod (you'll see this if there is no newer software available for your iPod).

   ◆ Option 2: Use Same Version – as option 1, but there is a more recent version of the iPod software available.

   ◆ Option 3: Use Newest Version – ignore the software on the iPod and restore using the most recent version of the iPod software available.

   ◆ Option 4: Restore and Update – essentially the same result as option 3.

5 If you are using a Macintosh and OS X, you'll have to enter your administrator's name and password in the dialogue box.

6 The restore will start. This is a two-stage process; at the end of the first stage you'll get one of the following two messages:

- For older iPod models: Disconnect iPod and connect it to iPod power adaptor.

- For more recent iPod models: Leave iPod connected to computer to complete restore.

7 During this second stage the iPod's display will show the Apple logo and a progress bar. Make sure the computer and iPod remain connected during this process; if you can't see the display clearly keep the two connected until a message appears in iTunes.

8 The iTunes Setup Assistant will appear at the end of the process and prompt you to give the iPod a name. Do this and also select the synchronizing preferences (this is the same as you would have done early on, when you set up your iPod for the first time).

9 Your iPod has now been reset and your preferences added. You can now download your media.

Restore: click on the Restore button in iTunes to start the process.

Step 6: Repaired?

Okay, so this isn't a sixth 'R'. Has your problem been solved by one of the previous steps? If yes, you can breathe a quiet sigh of relief and get back to enjoying your music, or videos. If no, it could be that you and your iPod need to visit an authorized repair centre. These will have all the diagnostic tools to put right what a run through of the five 'R's couldn't.

Before setting off, though, it might be worth reading through the rest of this section. We're going to take a look at some of the other fault conditions you might – rarely – see on your iPod.

What to do when Windows won't play ball (or music)

Both iTunes and the iPod were originally conceived for the Macintosh. The essential software was also first written with the Macintosh in mind as the hub of the system. However, for the iPod to become the global success it has it had to come to Windows PCs. And that poses problems, problems that beset all software designers. The Macintosh system is built around a tightly controlled hardware and software specification. No matter what Mac model you have its basic architecture is pretty similar to any other Mac.

In the Windows world with so many vendors and so many hardware component manufacturers there can be conflicts and inconsistencies. No matter how many permutations of hardware components and systems that software publishers try their test software on, there are likely to be some that the applications can be a bit flaky on.

In an attempt to pre-empt this, the Windows version of iTunes contains a feature called Diagnostics (**Help > Run Diagnostics**) that can help you overcome any potential problems. It includes diagnostic assistants for:

* **Network:** a series of tests to check that your computer's Internet connection is configured correctly, is up and running and able to access the iTunes Store.

* **iPod:** detects and diagnoses any potential problems in the connection between the iPod and the host computer.

- **CD/DVD:** diagnoses any problems with the import of music from disc or the export (and burning) of playlists to disc.

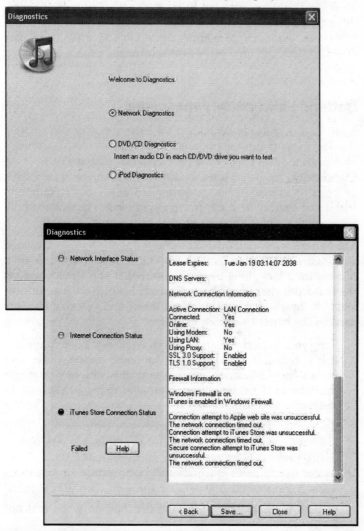

Windows Diagnostics: (top) the Windows-only diagnostics facility will let you diagnose problems with your network, iPod or CDs.

Diagnostics results: (bottom) the results of a diagnostics procedure are shown in the panel, along with a red light against any failures. Here the system has been unable to contact the iTunes Store.

On screen messages

Your iPod's screen can play host to a number of warning messages. Some are the sign of something serious happening, or about to happen. Some are more informative. Let's have a look at what you might see and how you might resolve any problem to which they allude.

Batteries and battery messages

Your iPod is crucially dependent on battery power. Fortunately the iPod uses lithium-ion batteries that, despite having commendable capacity, don't suffer the problems that plagued earlier battery chemistries. If you'd have used a video camera in the 1990s or before you'd have had to suffer NiCads – nickel cadmium batteries – that, to be used effectively, needed to be drained fully before rechargings. Topping up was an absolute no-no.

The batteries in your iPod can be charged at any time and, treated with just a modest amount of respect, should keep your iPod playing for a long, long time. To ensure that you will always get the best from your iPod's batteries and to assure the longest possible life, here are a few tips. Heed these, and you should never need to see battery warning messages:

- Keep your batteries charged – even if you don't use your iPod. If it is languishing in a drawer for some reason, make sure you top up the batteries every couple of weeks, or a month at the outside. This arrests any potential decay of the battery chemicals.

- Keep your iPod away from extremes of temperature. Apart from the security aspects, cars, for example, are very hostile environments. They get too hot in the sun and too cold on winter nights. Both extremes will compromise battery life.

- For extended playing sessions avoid power draining features such as the backlight or leaving the iPod on when it is not being used.

- Use a car power adaptor to keep your iPod fully charged when you're away from home and your computer.

As you use your iPod under its own power you'll see the battery icon on the screen on both the iPod and the iPod nano. As the power runs down the battery – initially coloured green on a full charge – will become progressively greyer. Eventually, when the battery is on the point of running out of power, the remaining green part will turn red. Then it's time to recharge; the iPod could shut down at any point.

Battery icons: the decreasing level here (shown for a fifth-generation iPod and iPod mini) correspond to the decreasing power.

If you ignored the red warning battery icon and carried on listening you'll reach the point where the iPod will shut down. There's just not enough power to carry on. Next time you try to start it, the iPod won't even have enough power to display a proper warning that its batteries are too low.

The battery icon: here displaying a full battery, half depleted and empty.

When it's in this state you'll obviously need to charge it – via the computer link or a mains/car adaptor – before you can even start it. Give it a good 30 minutes' charge before trying to start.

More warning icons and symbols

The battery icons are, for the most part purely informative, warning of low power. Top up the batteries and they'll make a discrete exit. Other icons and symbols may betray a more sinister problem.

Here are some along with the conditions they suggest:

The sad iPod: a sad iPod with a warning triangle. When connected to your computer the iPod neither appears in iTunes nor on the computer (that's in My Computer for Windows users or the Finder in OS X). Generally this indicates a hardware problem. If the iPod does not respond to any of the 5 'R's it will mean a trip to the service centre.

The sad iPod: generally a sign of a problem with your iPod's hardware.

The folder warning: a folder icon with a warning triangle. If you are using an iPod with a click wheel you may have the wrong software loaded. This may happen when you use your iPod for the first time on a Windows PC when you have not installed the software included with the iPod first. Remedy this by installing the iPod software from the CD first.

It can also appear when your battery charge is low. Use your computer connection or an external power adaptor to charge the iPod. If you are using a connection to a computer, ensure that during the charging process, the computer keeps awake. You generally won't be able to charge when the computer is asleep.

Folder warning: low power or a software incompatibility could lead to this worrying warning.

Do not disconnect: not always a sign of anything major, but one to obey. When your iPod is displaying this symbol disconnecting it from your computer could cause damage to the data on the iPod or, very exceptionally, on the host computer.

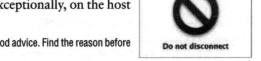

Do not disconnect: it's good advice. Find the reason before disconnecting.

If this symbol appears and you know that your iPod and computer are not communicating, try ejecting the iPod by either:

1   Pressing the **Eject** button adjacent to the iPod icon in the Sources window of iTunes.

2   Clicking the **Eject the iPod** icon on the desktop (Macintosh) or in **My Computer** (Windows).

Connect to power adaptor: you'll see this if it's important that you have a power connection (such as during an update or a system restore) but the iPod has detected that you don't have any charge flowing. It may be because the power socket to which you are connected is not turned on, or you have connected to a USB or FireWire connector that is not carrying power. You can rectify this problem by turning on the power at the socket, or connect the iPod to a powered socket on your computer.

Power warning: see this and you need to provide power ASAP.

Disc Icons: you'll see these icons if there's a problem with the hard disc of your iPod.

Disc scan: your iPod's hard disc is being scanned and checked. The bar below indicates progress.

 Scan failure: the disc scan failed and will be repeated the next time you turn it on.

 No problems found: the disc scan did not reveal any problems with the disc.

 Some problems found: ...but some were fixed.

 Scan cancelled: it will be repeated next time the iPod is switched on.

Battery replacement

The time will come, no matter how prudent and efficient you have been at extending the battery's life, when it will need replacing. The characteristics of a failing battery are obvious: it just won't last as long as it used to between charges. Early on this will be a little annoying; if it only plays for 12 hours between charges rather than 15 hours, that may be no big deal. But when that time drops to just an hour or two, it really is time for a change.

If this happens early on during your iPod's life (that is, within the first year) or within any extended warranty period (presuming the warranty covers the battery – not all do) you should return it for repair. If it's out of warranty, battery replacement through the authorized outlets can be expensive. In these cases you can find – thanks to Google or your favourite search engine – an online (or bricks-and-mortar) service depot that will exchange your battery for a more economic price.

Should you be willing (and able) then you can do it yourself. You'll find batteries available mail order if you are happy to open the case yourself – and know how to do so without causing damage. If you are in any doubt this is probably a job best left to the experts.

iPod battery pack: replacement batteries come complete – usually – with the specialist tool needed to open the iPod to gain access to the old battery.

Summary

As we said at the beginning, this is hopefully one chapter you won't need to read in earnest. However, it's good to be aware of the possible problem areas so you can avoid them. General advice to avoid trouble? Keep your batteries topped up, your software versions (for iPod and iTunes) up to date and follow the basic instructions for connecting. We can't guarantee you'll never have a problem but you'll certainly reduce the risks to a minimum.

resources

In this chapter you will learn:
- about digital music formats
- where you can find out more about iPods, iTunes and digital music
- where to find the latest (and coolest) iPod stuff
- how to make iTunes even better

The iPod can be compulsive. Not since the mobile phone has a device arrived that people have become so attached to. This is partly because it's such a neat device and partly because the content loaded on it can mean so much and, given our lifestyles, be so useful. In this book we've tried to give you a good grounding in what you need to know to get the best from your system; in this chapter we take a look at some more crucial information and where you can find out the latest info on iPods and iTunes. Also, we'll point you in the right direction to find out more information and even track down elusive – and free – music tracks.

Which file formats will work with your iPod and iTunes?

Let's begin by taking a look at the file formats that your iPod and iTunes can handle. Often this is rather inconsequential. If you rip your CD collection directly into iTunes and download others from the iTunes Store they will already be in the correct format. Visit some other music download sites and you may not be so lucky. You might also find that iTunes will – on occasions – not play some music. That's not necessarily down to a fault – we'll discover why in a moment.

Music file formats

Your iPod will support a number of music file formats including AAC, Protected AAC (that is, the digital rights managed tracks from the iTunes Store), MP3, Audible (audiobooks formats, 2, 3 and 4), Apple Lossless, AIFF and WAV. To use any other formats of music that you might acquire, you'll need to convert them to one of these first.

Problems with playing music files

Sometimes you'll have some music files in your library and they won't play. You may be absolutely sure that there is nothing wrong with them, so what is up?

If it's a song or album that you've downloaded from the iTunes Store, you might have exceeded the number of computers that have been authorized to play them, e.g. you authorized five and you are trying to play them on a sixth. Before you can play that music on your current computer you will have to deauthorize one of the existing ones. It's easy to get into this situation inadvertently, particularly if you upgrade your computer and don't deauthorize your old one before disposing of it.

You'll encounter a similar problem if you try to play music on a shared playlist (that is you are sharing someone else's library) and you have not been authorized to play music purchased by the owner of the list. To listen, you'll need to have the owner of the music authorize your computer.

If you are trying to play an AAC file created by a source other than iTunes itself or downloaded from the iTunes Store you will often have a problem. Files that are encoded into the AAC format by iTunes (and downloaded from the store) use the MPEG4 codec; other AAC files not produced using this codec are not supported and so won't play.

Converting file formats

You can use iTunes to convert your music tracks to different file formats. You might, for example want to save a copy of a compressed file format (such as MP3) into an uncompressed one, such as AIFF or WAV.

You can effect a conversion using the Preferences. Click on the Advanced tab and then click on Importing. Select the encoding format that you want to convert your music to.

Now, in the main iTunes library select the tracks you want to convert. Select **Advanced > Convert Selection to AAC** (or whichever file format you want to convert the music to).

When you make a copy of a file in this way, monitor the quality of the sound in the new file. Normally you won't have any problems – soundwise – when you copy a compressed file format to an uncompressed one, but copying one compressed format to another (such as MP3 to AAC) can compromise the quality of music. To avoid any degradation, it will be better to re-import the music tracks from the original, uncompressed sources, if at all possible.

Video and image files

iTunes will support video files that end with the .mov, .m4v or .mp4 file extensions. It will also support images in the formats JPEG, TIFF, PSD, BMP, GIF, SGI, PNG, PICT and JPG2000, though compatibility with image files does depend to a degree on the iTunes version and whether you are using it on a PC or a Macintosh.

Finding out more about iTunes and iPods

If you want to find out more about iTunes and iPods – including the latest developments and rated guides to the latest accessories – you'll find a number of websites there to cater for you. There are even some physical publications – monthly magazines – now devoted to the duo.

'Surprised', 'Disappointed', 'Amazed'. If you want to keep abreast of all that's happening in the world of iPods and iTunes be prepared to experience all three. Surprised? Apple keeps things very much to its chest and few genuine secrets appear ahead of any launch. Disappointed? Sometimes; if you latch on to all the rumour sites you'll be expecting the next iPod to do everything your laptop does, and more besides; and at a knock-down price. Reality is often more realistic. Amazed? Almost certainly. Take the iPhone. The original phone solution was, as we mentioned earlier, rather underwhelming, yet the iPhone itself blew away everyone who saw it. Keeping an eye on the Web can keep you abreast of what is happening with iPods and iTunes. Some of it is definitive news, some speculation. But, as part of the iPod phenomenon you're likely to find all of it compelling.

Information websites

Here are a few websites that provide general, and specific, advice on your iPod and iTunes and that you might want to add to your favourites:

Apple: www.apple.com/itunes. Something of a portal to everything officially connected with iPods and iTunes with links to the products and resources. Coming from the mouth of Apple it doesn't tend to speculate on future products and also is slanted towards product sales but it is a good place for definitive information. Apple also have a very comprehensive set of technical documents that you can peruse if you need to find out something specific, or want to diagnose problems.

Apple's iPod website: everything about the iPod that's official.

EverythingiPod: www.everythingipod.com – a great independent source of information and technical support. Just as useful if you've an old iPod or the latest.

iLounge: www.ilounge.com – another totally independent and very comprehensive site that also features support information, user guides and forums for iPod users to exchange news and views.

Everything iPod (top): that's an awful lot – but this website covers it well.
iLounge (bottom): a great independent resource on the iPod, its family and friends.

Rumour sites

The Internet is awash with rumour websites on just about every-thing, so it should come as no surprise that with its popularity and the high general interest levels, the iPod features in a great many. Given that it was spawned by the same company that produced the Macintosh, most of these sites are offshoots of Apple or Macintosh fan sites.

iPodRumors: ipod.macrumors.com – like many rumour sites, much of what you'll read is mere speculation but this site does have a good track record of accurate news too. You just have to guess which ones are so.

ThinkSecret: www.thinksecret.com – a Macintosh rumour site with a strong focus on the iPod and iTunes.

General technology sites

To find out where the iPod and iTunes sit in the world of tech-nology, and what the guys at Apple might be seeing over their shoulders there are some great general technology websites out there aggregating information from across the world. You'll have to dig a bit deeper for specific news items but the results will generally be more objective, on the basis that they are not writ-ten – necessarily – by iPod converts. Here are a few to scan, or to add their newsfeeds to your aggregator:

+ **The Inquirer:** www.theinquirer.net
+ **Coolest Gadgets:** www.coolest-gadgets.com
+ **Gizmodo:** www.gizmodo.com
+ **T3:** www.t3.co.uk
+ **Engadget:** www.engadget.com

Music websites

The iTunes Store has become so comprehensive in its coverage that most people have little reason to go anywhere else for their music. However, no matter how extensive the library of tracks, there will always be some music that is outside the iTunes um-brella. It might be that the music is new and not yet established, or it's very specialized music, or it may even be that the writers or performers don't want to be part of iTunes. The good news is that no matter how abstract or bizarre your musical tastes, you'll be very unlucky if you can't track down the music somewhere. Better still, some new and emerging acts are so keen to let you hear – and hopefully enjoy – their music that they will give you their music for free; there are sites too that gather together this music and deliver it free of charge. You can find these by searching on 'free music download sites' but here are a couple to get you started:

Jamendo: www.jamendo.com – a popular place for free music that allows unlimited downloads and also allows artists to upload their music too.

AltSounds: www.altsounds.com – a good place not only to discover new bands and music but also to find music videos and photographs.

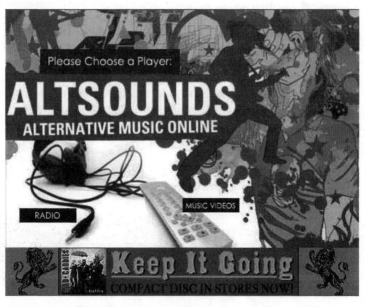

Altsounds.com: if it's not on iTunes give Altsounds a go.

iTunes plug-ins: making a good thing better?

If you are a devotee of an application such as Photoshop you will probably already be aware of plug-ins. These are small programs that – as the name might suggest – plug in to the host to extend the functionality. In Photoshop you can find hundreds – thousands – of plug-ins that mostly add additional special effect features for enhancing images.

Now iTunes too is gathering interest from musical programmers keen to extend the functionality beyond that which Apple currently offers. You can use your favourite search engine to track some of these down or pay a visit to PluginsWorld (http://itunes.pluginsworld.com) to find a comprehensive listing. Here you'll also find some ratings from users and also whether they are commercial (that is, you'd have to pay for them) or freeware (when they are free but the author may appreciate a nominal donation to keep the work going).

Here are some interesting free ones:

- **iLyrics:** (Windows only) finds and imports song lyrics into your iTunes library.

- **Soundcrank:** adds album artwork and lyrics to your iTunes music library and can show you what your friends are listening to.

- **The Filter:** a powerful plug-in that scans and analyses your iTunes library to help you create intelligent playlists in real time based on your musical preferences.

The Filter: this neat application integrates well with iTunes and allows you to create powerful playlists.

Final comments

This is where our adventure with the iPod and iTunes ends – for now. One thing that you probably have realized is that the iPod and iTunes have come a long way since their arrival at the turn of the century and that they will continue to evolve. As you are reading this you may be using a newer version of the iPod or downloading the latest version of iTunes.

Both these products have achieved much of their success because they are easy to use and deliver results that exceed our expectations. The whole world has been seduced and hooked on a single device that has enabled us to carry our music, photos and videos with us everywhere. We see the trademark white earpieces everywhere and now, with the iPhone, the reach of the iPod has extended even further. The iPod family is the source of tremendous power – and it's all within your reach!

AAC (Advanced Audio Coding): A compression format for digital audio used by Apple for the iTunes Music Store and offering much higher quality than the original MP3 format. AAC was developed as part of the standard for the video format MPEG4 used for high-quality audio and video on the Web, and some digital television broadcasts. Often uses the .M4A file extension.

ADC: Analogue-to-digital converter: an electronic system that may be part of a computer, a peripheral attached to a computer or a stand-alone device designed to convert an analogue signal to a digital one. This may be used to convert analogue audio to digital, analogue video to digital video, according to need. Used in reverse it becomes a digital-to-analogue converter or DAC.

AIFF (.aiff): The original and default sound file on Macintosh computers.

Analogue: A non-digital signal recorded from real-world sources. Rather than representing all the data in an audio or video file as a precise digital code the analogue signal represents the data as a continuously varying signal. Although this is a true representation, it is difficult to copy: copies of an original analogue recording will progressively degrade, whereas digital data can be copied almost indefinitely.

Analogue-to-digital converter: *see* ADC.

Apple Lossless: Apple Lossless Encoding (also known as ALE, Apple Lossless and Apple Lossless Audio Codec). The audio encoding system or codec developed by Apple Computer and capable of providing full, CD-quality audio without loss but in around half the space of the original file. It is proprietary to

Apple Inc. and normally will only function through iTunes (on Windows or Macintosh PCs) and through Quicktime. There is an equivalent open source (i.e. non-proprietary) version called FLAC.

ATRAC™: Audio file format developed by Sony, originally in the early 1990s and offering near-CD audio quality. It was devised so that a whole CD of audio could be accommodated on the then-new Sony MiniDisc format.

ATRAC3™: An evolution of the ATRAC codec that uses even greater compression but with little loss of quality. It is used by some MiniDisc recorders and for audio storage in (mainly Sony) portable memory players. Some online Internet music applications like Liquid Audio and RealAudio also use this format.

Audible: A digital file format principally used for acoustically undemanding roles such as for spoken word files and almost exclusively for files and audio resources purchased from the Audible.com website. Audible files are available with four compression rates – Audible 1 is the most compressed and 4 the least. iPods use this format for files downloaded from Audible, but only in compressions 2 and 4. The benefit of this format is bookmarking: ensuring that if you are listening to a long audio book your position is not lost if you stop and later return.

Audible.com: A source of voice recordings and audio books that use the Audible format. Purchases from the Audible store are compatible with most digital music players and all computers.

Audio compression: *see* Compression.

Audio frequency (AF): Sound frequencies that are within the standard or normal range of unimpaired human hearing. This is usually defined as between 20Hz and 20,000Hz (20kHz). 1Hz (Hertz) is one vibration per second.

Audio Player: *see* Digital audio player.

Audiocast: Audio content broadcast over the Internet. It's a general term that can describe streamed audio, podcasts, DAB broadcasts and any other audio-only source.

Audiophile: Person who has a wish for the highest quality sound.

Audiophile components/hardware: Hifi components that meet the demanding needs of audiophiles.

Auxiliary input: A cable input that enables you to connect an iPod (or any other audio device) to an amplifier, receiver or other replay device. The cable traditionally features a phono (RCA) connector but in the case of digital audio players is likely to be a minijack termination at one end and the proprietary connection (such as an iPod dock) at the other.

Bit rate: The number of digital data bits (discrete 1s or 0s comprising the digital data signal) transmitted or recorded in one second. The higher the bit rate, the better the sound reproduction. The average number of bits that one second of audio data will consume. Standard digital music bit rates are 64kbps (kilobits per second), 96kbps, 128kbps, and 160kbps. Higher bit rates are also offered in some file formats.

Bits per second (bps): *see* Bit rate.

Blog: Short for weblog, normally a personal diary/journal designed for widespread reading and comment over the Internet. Blogs generally take the form of individual entries that are listed in reverse time order, with the most recent addition at the top.

Blu Ray: Disc format popularized and supported by media companies including Apple and Sony and designed to accommodate large data quantities and high definition recordings. Promoted as the successor to DVD.

Burn: The process of writing data to a recordable optical disc such as Blu Ray, DVD, CD-R, or CD-RW.

Burn proof: Contraction of 'Buffer underrun proof', a technology that prevents problems associated with interruptions to the data flow when CDs are recorded (resulting in disc failure). It ensures that sufficient data is held in memory, or a buffer, to ensure a continuous supply to the recording system.

Cassette adapter: A modified compact cassette housing which allows you to listen to your iPod or other digital music player through the cassette player in your car. A connection is run from the iPod (using the headphone socket or dock) to the adaptor.

CD Database, CDDB: *see* Gracenote Media Recognition Service.

CD-Recordable (CD-R): A conventional recordable CD suitable for recording data (for computer use) and music/audio for playing in CD players. Data (of any kind) can only be recorded in a single session.

CD-Rewritable (CD-RW): Similar to a CD-R but offers the opportunity to re-record. These discs can be used for music/audio recordings but their compatibility is not always as great as CDs or CD-Rs. Often CD-RW discs can only read by CD-RW drives and sometimes will only replay in the original drive used to record.

Click wheel: A control used on Apple iPod models and also on some telephones made by Bang and Olufsen. In the iPod, the wheel allows fast scrolling through menus and (by pressing the appropriate point) Menu, Fast-Forward, Rewind, and Play/Pause buttons. Original click wheels rotated physically, whereas later ones are fixed and touch-sensitive, which avoids potential problems due to wear.

Codec: A contraction of the term compression/decompression. Codecs are mathematical rules that, when applied to a file, transform its type. Codecs are applied behind the scenes when you, for example, import a CD to your library – the original music files will be converted to, say AAC through the use of an appropriate codec.

Compact Disc Audio, CD-A: The format of audio on a standard commercial music CD. Though digital, the files are not very compact and need to be compressed if any quantity is to be stored on a digital music device. Also, the files need to be converted to a format such as WAV or AIFF for playing on a computer.

Compression: A process of reducing the size of a digital file (applies to audio, video or photo files) to make it more compact and enable more files to be included on a specific media. There are a range of compression types (such as AAC, MP3) available; each offers a different variation on the compression/quality ratio. Compression generally works by identifying and removing those frequencies that are not normally audible to the human ear or do not contribute significantly to the music. Lossless compression systems compress files without losing or discarding data.

Constant Bit Rate (CBR): A type of data encoding that uses a steady stream of data supplied at a fixed bit rate. The same amount of data is recorded irrespective of the complexity of the music or audio being recorded. This can result in poorer quality sound, particularly in detailed parts of the music. Compare with Variable Bit Rate.

DAB (Digital Audio Broadcasting): A standard and technology for the broadcast of audio over digital radio. The objective of DAB is to provide higher audio quality (though quality can be affected by compression and the use of low bit rates), less interference, and a more robust signal. The overriding driver for DAB, however, is the ability, as with digital television, to offer more stations/channels in a given amount of radio frequency spectrum (that is, the portion of radio frequencies available for radio transmission).

Digital audio player: 1. Software found on a computer for the replay of digital music, such as iTunes or Windows Media Player. 2. General term for a portable device for the replay of digital music such as an iPod, Zune or Zen.

Digital radio: *see* DAB.

Digital Rights Management (DRM): Technology designed to protect any digital media or resource from unauthorized copying or distribution. Because digital copies of resources can be as good as the original, theft of the copyright and intellectual property is easy. Media or resources that have DRM embedded in the files may feature restrictions on the copying and distribution. For example, DRM may allow a purchased music track to be copied to another authorized computer, but not used with a music distribution system. AAC and WMA formats can support DRM.

Digital Versatile Disc (DVD): Sometimes (erroneously) described as a digital video disc, an optically read disc with the capacity of holding up to 9GB of data per side. Normally used for video and movie content but also suitable for computer data storage.

Digitizing, digitization: The process of converting analogue data and information into a digital form. This is normally achieved by using an analogue-to-digital converter, or digitizer.

Disc-at-once (DAO): Recording method used for the creation of CDs where all the data to be written is added in a single session; once initiated, the disc burning process cannot be interrupted and no further data can be added to the disc even if there is space.

Dock: A cradle for the iPod (and some other digital music players) that connects to a computer for charging the battery and transferring songs. Some docks also allow connection to a TV or hifi for the replay of respective media. Mini docks are small plugs that connect a cable to an iPod without the physical docking and are used (mainly) for portable connections.

Dock connector: The port on an iPod that connects it to a dock and provides connectivity for charging, music input/output and video input/output where available.

Encoder: A software application with or without associated hardware that can convert one audio file format into another. For example, an AAC encoder will convert a WAV file into an AAC file.

File format: A specific arrangement and structure of digital data within a file. A file format provides data in a form that applications and devices can recognize and use. With regard to digital music, AIFF, WAV, MP3 and AAC are amongst the most widespread formats.

Filter: Used to modify an incoming sound or audio file to limit, for example, the high frequencies; used in digital music applications to assist in the removal of elements of music when compressing a file.

FireWire®: Also called IEEE 1394 or i.LINK®, the latter with Sony devices, FireWire is a fast (up to 400 megabits per second), two-way digital connection used between a computer and peripherals, including some iPods. Newer iPods use the marginally faster USB 2 connection system.

Firmware: An operating system and associated software installed on an electronic device. Normally it is stored on memory chips and is only indirectly accessible by the users, though it can be upgraded to add additional functionality.

FLAC: An open-source codec for compressing audio, broadly similar to Apple Lossless Compression. No audio data is lost in the compression process but the amount of compression (at around 50%) is less than codecs that discard some data.

Flash memory: A type of memory used in computers and peripherals, including music players, cameras, phones and video cameras, that retains information when the device is switched off and also when power is disconnected. Proprietary applications include memory cards such as SD cards and Compactflash.

Flash memory is valued in digital music players because it has no moving parts and will not jump or skip during the replay of music.

Free Lossless Audio Codec: *see* FLAC.

Gracenote Media Recognition Service: Formerly called CDDB – CD Database – is a CD and media recognitions service used by various services including iTunes. Your computer can interrogate the database when uploading a CD to your music player and automatically acquire all the track and album names. The content of the database is supplied by users themselves and then checked and reconciled by Gracenote.

Hard drive: Small rotating disc (or discs) used for magnetic data storage in a computer and high-capacity digital music players. Hard discs are less robust than flash memory but are cheaper on a per gigabyte basis. To avoid skipping due to movement, the hard discs used in devices such as iPods include a buffer to store several minutes' music to allow the disc to catch up.

Hertz (Hz): The unit of measurement of both electrical vibrations (cycles) and sound wave vibrations, per second. One Hz is equal to one vibration or cycle per second.

ID3, ID3 Tag: Data encoded in a digital music file that contains information such as track details, titles, artist and more. Using software music players such as iTunes, this information can be changed and modified. The music player uses the tagged information to identify music.

IEEE 1394: *see* FireWire.

i.Link ®: *see* FireWire.

iPhone: Device combining an iPod, mobile telephone and mobile Internet device. Enhanced interface and display features are borrowed from iTunes.

iPod: Brand name and device name of the range of digital music players launched by Apple Inc. (then Apple Computer Inc.) in 2001. The single name 'iPod' also describes the flagship product of the iPod range, now dubbed the iPod Classic. The range also features the iPod nano (a cut down, smaller, lower-capacity version that uses flash memory exclusively), the iPod shuffle (a very small, low-capacity version with no display) and the iPhone-inspired iPod Touch. It has also been used for the iPod mini, essentially an iPod nano that used a micro hard drive rather than flash memory.

iPod mini: *see* iPod.

iPod nano: *see* iPod.

iPod shuffle: *see* iPod.

iPod Touch: *see* iPod.

iTunes®, iTunes Music Store: The music storage, organizing and management facility for Windows and Mac PCs along with the tightly integrated music and movie download store. iTunes is also tightly integrated with the iPod, and synchronizes with the latter whenever attached. TV shows, movies, podcasts, audio books and games can also be downloaded from the store and included in the iTunes library.

iTunes+, iTunes Plus: Term used by Apple to refer to songs and music videos provided through the iTunes Music Store at high quality (256kbps data rate) and using AAC encoding. More significantly, it does not feature DRM. Songs purchased from iTunes Plus command a price premium; music previously purchased can be upgraded for a nominal amount.

iTunes U: U stands for University – this part of the iTunes Music Store provides learning resources that can be downloaded to iTunes and, where relevant, iPods.

iTunes WiFi Music Store: A version of the iTunes Store designed to allow access to music for downloading over a WiFi network, direct to an iPod Touch or iPhone.

Jukebox, digital jukebox: A music or video player that can play a sequence of random or predetermined tracks (or video resources) in the same way as a traditional vinyl disc jukebox. Sometimes used as a generic term for digital music players that use playlists to order and schedule music replays.

Minidock: *see* Dock.

MP3: Short for MPEG-1, Audio Layer 3, this popular digital audio compression format reduces the size of audio files. Now superseded by many other formats (that tend to offer better quality), MP3s reduce file sizes by discarding unnecessary data that is essentially inaudible to a typical human ear. However, audiophiles do tend to acknowledge the poor quality and claim to be able to detect the difference. A typical MP3 file will be around one tenth the size of an original WAV file.

MP3 player: A term normally used to describe a digital music player (hardware or software) even though that hardware or software may handle digital files of a different type; iPods are often called MP3 players, even though they do not play MP3 files.

Multi-session: CD recording system that allows data to be written to a CD in several separate sessions. Unlike Disc at once (DAO), data can be added until the disc is full. However, before the disc can be played in a conventional CD player it must be finalized. This adds a table of contents (TOC) to the disc, essentially a directory that tells a computer or CD player where to find tracks and data.

Normalize, normalization: A process applied to audio recordings that increases or decreases the amplitude of the sound waves and normally used to boost the sound levels to the maximum permitted by the recording medium but without introducing distortion. Often used to make best use of the bandwidth for a digital file or audio CD and to make the sound appear louder.

Ogg Vorbis: An open source (i.e. non-proprietary) codec that can be freely used to encode audio without incurring licensing costs. It is a lossy compression system that, like MP3, discards some audio data in order to produce a more compact file. Although it is debatable, proponents of Ogg Vorbis contend that the algorithms used to encode are more efficient than MP3 and can produce more compact files (or better quality for a given file size). The name comes from 'ogging' (a term from the computer game Netrek) and the Discworld character, Exquisitor Vorbis.

Party shuffle: A feature of iTunes (and similar features can be found in other applications) that automatically selects the upcoming songs from an iTunes library or playlists. Users can delete or juggle upcoming songs at any point. Designed for party and background music applications.

Peer-based file sharing: A software-driven system that allows large numbers of files to be shared using individual computers as hosts, rather than a central fileserver. Used by the original (subsequently deemed illegal) Napster music sharing service, an organization not connected with the current Napster service.

Playlist: A custom group of individual music tracks gathered together (manually or automatically) from a larger digital music library for playing directly or downloading to a digital music player.

Playsforsure: Microsoft certification for software and hardware, including that designed to support digital music, that assures interoperability. Certified devices support WMA and Windows Media DRM.

Podcast: A digital media file (conventionally audio but also video) that can be distributed over the Internet and that allows users to subscribe to regular episodic updates. You can subscribe to podcasts either directly from a website or via an application such as iTunes.

Podcaster: The author, host or originator of a podcast.

Podcatcher: A computer-based application that automatically checks predetermined web locations for podcast feeds and then automatically downloads any new items.

Ripping: The process of extracting the audio tracks from a CD, for example, and converting them to a format that can be loaded to an application such as iTunes. Also used to describe the process of getting DVD content (principally video) from the disc and loaded onto a computer. This normally requires that the original DVD is not copy-protected.

Sampling rate: A sample is a snapshot of the audio data at a particular time. It contains all the relevant information about the music at that precise instant. The sample rate defines how many are taken each second and is measured in kHz (kilohertz). Clearly the more that are recorded per second, the more authentic the replay will be. The sampling rate for CD audio is a little over 44kHz.

Server-based file sharing: File sharing process where all the files to be shared are stored on one or more central servers rather than, as in peer-to-peer serving, the individual users' computers.

Shuffle: *see* iPod.

Streaming audio: Live or pre-recorded audio that is downloaded from the Internet, and which starts playing while it continues to download. The format is used by many Internet radio stations.

The downloaded media are not normally stored on the receiving computer.

Table of Contents (TOC): *see* Multi-session.

Track: A single session of music or audio on CD or digital music player that is identified as such and which a user can jump to the start of.

Track-at-once (TAO): An alternative recording method for CDs (compared with Disc-at-once) that can write tracks individually to a CD and will separate each by a gap of a couple of seconds. Normally up to 99 tracks can be added to a single disc.

USB: Universal Serial Bus – an interface/connection used by computers to connect to peripherals such as printers, keyboards and mice. Many digital music players also use one to synchronize with the music software on the host computer. The data communications run at 480 Mbps in USB 2. USB 2 is backwards compatible with the much slower original USB 1.1 standard.

Variable Bit Rate (VBR): A method of recording audio signals that allows the rate of recording of digital data to vary according to the needs of the digital content. For complex passages of music where more detail is required, the bit rate will increase to maintain quality; in less complex parts the data rate can be reduced without reducing or compromising quality. Compare with Constant Bit Rate.

Video podcasting: A form of podcasting that uses video files rather than audio; sometimes called vodcasting, vidcasting or vlogging.

Vorbis: *see* Ogg Vorbis.

WAV: The Microsoft sanctioned standard for digital sound files that produces high quality sound, but in files that are larger than those in MP3 format.

Wireless FM transmitter: A small FM transmitter that connects to an iPod (or other digital music device) and broadcasts its output at a predetermined FM radio frequency. This allows a car driver to tune the car radio to the corresponding frequency and listen to the music as if it were a broadcast radio station. It is 'wireless' both in terms of radio frequency and in that it doesn't need to be hard-wired into the car. The quality is not as good as a hard-wired system and these can be prone to interference.

WMA: Windows Media Audio (WMA) is the name for a group of Microsoft-developed audio file formats. WMA Standard is similar to AAC and Ogg Vorbis. The more recent AAC Professional is a newer, more efficient format (producing better sound quality with smaller file sizes). WMA Lossless is a lossless format for specialized use. There is also a voice-optimized format, WMA Voice.

Zen: A range of digital audio players and portable media players produced by Creative Technology.

Zune: The umbrella name for Microsoft's digital audio player, the music library/management software and online music store (Zune Marketplace). The early Zune players included FM radio and had wireless connectivity for sharing files and music. The player can also connect with Xbox 360s.

index